# profiles in black

## PHAT FACTS FOR TEENS

**MARVIN A. McMICKLE**

Jean Alicia Elster, editor

Foreword by Efrem Smith

## JUDSON PRESS
**PUBLISHERS SINCE 1824**

VALLEY FORGE, PA

PROFILES IN BLACK: PHAT FACTS FOR TEENS

The author and Judson Press have made every effort to ensure the accuracy of all facts.
In the event of a question arising from the information contained herein, we regret any
error made and will be pleased to make the necessary correction in future printings
and editions of this book.

Library of Congress Cataloging-in-Publication Data
McMickle, Marvin Andrew.
Profiles in black: Phat facts for teens / Marvin A. McMickle; Jean Alicia Elster, editor.
— 1st ed.
p. cm.
ISBN 978-0-8170-1508-4 (pbk. : alk. paper) 1. African Americans—History—
Juvenile literature. 2. African Americans—Biography—Juvenile literature. 3.
Christian youth—Education—United States. I. Elster, Jean Alicia. II. Title.
E185.M373 2008
973'.0496073—dc22

2008005903

Printed on recycled paper in the U.S.A.
First Edition, 2008.

# Contents

# Foreword

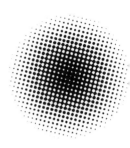

## Hip Hop and History: A Much Needed Connection

I grew up in the church and in hip hop. These two streams have had a tremendous impact on my life as they shaped my professional calling as a pastor, writer, and artist. I've been called by some "the hip-hop preacher," but I prefer "the hip-hop theologian." The reason I prefer the latter is because I think it's important for the hip-hop generation to present their skills, talents, and abilities but to do so in the context of knowing our history, that we might make a positive contribution to society. This is why growing up both in hip hop and in the church is so important.

Hip hop represents my voice, my passion, and my audacity to say what is on my heart and in my spirit no matter what. My preaching, singing, and shouting are influenced by hip-hop culture, which is influenced by James Brown and George Clinton. The funk is the roots of hip hop, and along with the influences of spoken-word artist such as The Last Poets, hip hop is an urban subculture. It's a culture for more reasons than just funk music and spoken-word poetry though. It's a culture because pioneers such as D.J. Kool Herc, D.J. Hollywood, and the hip-hop philosopher Afrika Bambaataa had ideas beyond just music. Hip-hop culture is based on the principles of peace, love, unity, community, and having fun. It is made up of five elements which are the DJ, the MC, the break-dancer (also known as the b-boy or b-girl), and the often unmentioned, knowledge of God and knowledge of self. The roots of funk and spoken word combined with the original principles and elements are what make hip hop the now multiethnic and global super-culture that it is today. Can you feel what I'm saying? An urban subculture, started by mostly African American youth, has now become a multiethnic super-culture influencing youth around the world!

When I wrote *The Hip-Hop Church* with Pastor Phil Jackson of Chicago, I never would have thought that we would receive e-mail from Russia, South Africa, and the UK, but we did. The problem today is that many young people listen to commercial rap music, but they don't know the history, principles, and elements of hip-hop culture. This is why to be a true hip-hopper one must borrow the biblical phrase, "study to show thyself approved" (2 Timothy 2:15). This is why growing up in the church as well as hip hop is so important.

Growing up in the church helped me become a responsible member of the hip-hop generation. How? First and most importantly because I learned about God. (Remember the element of hip hop that is knowledge of God and knowledge of self.) To truly know who I was as a member of the hip-hop generation and to know my calling within the culture, I needed to know God personally through Jesus Christ and through the indwelling of the Holy Spirit. Second, it was in the African American church that I learned African American history. The African American church is not just a place of singing, preaching, and shouting. It's not just a place where service starts at 10:00 on Sunday morning and lets out around 1:30 in the afternoon. It's a community of empowerment, leadership development, and history.

There is a need for a marriage between the African American church and the urban subculture of hip hop and its African American history. Maybe the better metaphor for the relationship is adoption. History must *adopt* hip hop because without it hip hop is an orphan. That's why this book, *Profiles in Black: Phat Facts for Teens* is so important. We need to present African American history in a relevant way to the second generation of hip hop. Many young people today feel disconnected from the church and from their history. In part, we as adults must take responsibility for this, and that is exactly what Rev. Dr. Marvin A. McMickle has done by writing this book. He is taking responsibility and bringing history to young people so that they may be empowered by the knowledge they receive from this book. He lays out African American history in a practical and readable fashion, but he also challenges young readers who are willing to engage this book as well. He does a great job in connecting the early history of slavery, Jim Crow segregation, and the early days of hip hop. This is the first time

History must adopt hip hop because without
it hip hop is an orphan.

that I've had the privilege of reading a book which intentionally connects slavery with the civil rights movement and hip-hop culture. McMickle's young readers will read *Profiles in Black* and not only learn about their elders, but they will see themselves as well. Thank you, my brother, for showing so much love for the hip-hop culture by writing this book!

Of course, the hip-hop generation must take responsibility as well. Take responsibility by reading this volume and taking seriously the rich information within it. Let this book make you a responsible member of the hip-hop culture. There should be no way that you can read this book and degrade women, see violence as the primary way to solve conflict, or glorify a "gangsta" lifestyle. As a preacher I desire to present a word that speaks in a relevant way to young people but also incorporates the history of black preaching that I observed and absorbed as a youth. In this way I show love for hip hop and great respect for my elders at the same time. This book performs that simultaneous act on paper. The greater purpose of each one of us is to honor God by practicing this simultaneous act in every aspect of our life. Read this book and allow our history as a people and your connection to God equip you to be a young hero who makes a positive impact in the world around you right now.

—Efrem Smith, Pastor
Sanctuary Covenant Church
Minneapolis, Minnesota
Author, *Raising Up Young Heroes*
and *The Hip-Hop Church*

# Preface

"Those who do not learn from history are destined to repeat it." Those are the words of the Spanish-born American philosopher George Santana. Nothing is more important to the future of a people or a nation than a clear understanding of their past and of the roads and struggles that have led to any present moment. History does not begin with any present generation and then work its way toward the future. History involves our acute awareness of the people and events that preceded us into the world and that must inform us as we seek to live in and give shape to the days and years that stretch out before us.

This book is offered with such a view of history in mind. Every African American in particular and all Americans in general are the beneficiaries of the people and events that are discussed in this book. It must never be forgotten that a centuries-long legacy of slavery and segregation continues to inform much of American life to this day. The better we understand those issues, and the more keenly we understand just how recently they have been legally overturned, the better we will be able to deal with their lasting effects.

Millions of African Americans alive today were impacted by Jim Crow laws, segregation policies, "separate but equal" public facilities, and the exclusion of African American people from whole sections of American life. We cannot write a better and brighter future for our nation unless and until we fully understand how dark and how very difficult our past has been as a people and as a nation. This book is intended to shed some light on the struggles and achievements of the past, in the hope that these stories and biographies can inspire in this and in future generations of Americans the courage to resist the downward pull of racism and to persist in the pursuit of a more just society.

This book is not meant simply to document the problems that have presented themselves over the last nearly four hundred years; the

*In every generation, and from one century to the next,
the men and women and young people...pursued
their dreams until they came true.*

primary mission of this book is to celebrate those persons and movements that refused to allow the racism at work in others to set limits on their hopes and dreams. The people whose stories are told in this book did not simply sing "We Shall Overcome" as a wish for the future. These people were busy overcoming what many may have viewed as insurmountable barriers. In every generation, and from one century to the next, the men and women and young people documented in this book overcame slavery, fear, intimidation, poverty, self-doubt, and a general lack of public support and/or encouragement. They pursued their dreams until they came true.

Think of the religious leaders who rejected the inherited readings of the Bible that pointed to black inferiority and that justified slavery and second-class citizenship. They reread and reworked the Scriptures and fashioned a new understanding of the will and ways of God. Think of the civil rights leaders and volunteers who marched and protested in parts of the country that were infested with the hate-filled presence of the Ku Klux Klan. Those persons simply marched into the face of that hatred and sang as they went, "We shall not be moved."

Think of the athletes who left the safety of numbers and stepped onto the playing field or the boxing ring or the tennis court by themselves in the face of racist slurs and resentment. Think of the scientists, the scholars, the lawyers, the artists, and the other trailblazers whose stories are recorded in the pages that follow. Every one of them overcame great odds, and every one of them made a great contribution to the nation and to the world. Think of the white people who put their lives at risk to become heralds of justice for their African American brothers and sisters. Think of the legal struggles that resulted in actions by the United States Congress, the president of the United States, or the United States Supreme Court. These things did not just happen; these legal actions were the result of the measures taken by men and women whose stories are told in this book.

Keep this truth in mind as you read the pages that follow. These are the stories that document a large portion of African American history. These are a sampling of the men and women, and these are a listing of some of the movements that have given shape to American life as we know it today. This book is not meant to be the exhaustive and definitive treatment of all aspects of African American life and achievement. Instead, it is a sampling, a survey of African American history. More important, it is primarily intended for young readers or for those whose knowledge of African American history is still being shaped.

Those who are experts in the field will be familiar with everything that is recorded here and may wish for more. This book is not written with that level of expertise in mind but is intended rather for those who have not been exposed to the breadth and depth of the African American story. It is written in chronological order rather than in narrative form so that the reader can see how history has unfolded over time. Sometimes the courage of those who are discussed here can better be grasped when one realizes how difficult were the times in which they lived.

The chronological order will also allow readers to see that the push for freedom did not begin with the modern civil rights movement of the 1950s and 1960s. From the time that Africans were brought to America, the desire to live free has been at work. Sometimes that desire took the form of peaceful demonstrations and nonviolent forms of resistance. Other times, especially when slavery was the enemy that needed to be addressed, nonviolence proved not to be the weapon of choice.

Prepare yourself to see individual and solitary acts of courage. Prepare yourself to see people coming together to throw off the bonds and boundaries that had long limited their hopes and dreams. Prepare yourself to see hundreds of years of American history unfold in the lives and struggles of heroic and selfless men, women, and children. Remember these stories and the people whose lives are recorded here. Whatever the future may hold for America in the twenty-first century, all of us can say that we have come this far by faith—and these profiles in black are a testimony to the travails and triumphs that will carry us forward into the next generation.

# Acknowledgments

I want to express my deep appreciation to the many people whose help and encouragement have made this book possible. I am grateful for my mother, Marthetta McMickle, who set my life on a path of reading before I even started school. Her example and her encouragement have nurtured me to become a reader, which is the first step on the road to becoming a writer. She died in 2005, but her legacy of love for reading will be continued by everyone who reads this book.

I want to thank African American historians, such as John Hope Franklin, Lerone Bennett Jr., and Vincent Harding, who demonstrated the various models and methods by which history can be viewed and taught. They have been my teachers even though I never took a class from any of them. Their many books and articles were my meat and milk during the formative years of my life. The fact that all of them are alive as this book is being published is a special blessing. My efforts here are largely a tribute to their scholarly contributions that have informed my view of history.

I thank God that I grew up in an interesting time and had the privilege of living in interesting places. I was born in Chicago in 1948, a city that had been founded by a black man. I had the privilege of living in the city where so much African American history and culture were shaped. The sounds of the blues, jazz, gospel, and R&B flowed all around me as a youth. My first barber was a member of Muhammad's Mosque #2, which was two blocks from my house. I watched black baseball players integrate the Chicago Cubs and the Chicago White Sox. They were making history before my eyes. Martin Luther King Jr. brought the civil rights movement to Chicago in 1966 for an open housing campaign. That movement had little if any effect on Chicago, but it changed my life forever. I was greatly aided in writing this book simply by being born in Chicago.

I am equally indebted to the city of New York, where I lived for some time, and to the city of Cleveland, where I now reside. Much of what is in this book is commentary on things I learned from those cities. I worked at Abyssinian Baptist Church for four years. I knew Samuel Dewitt Proctor, and I learned about Adam Clayton Powell Sr. and Adam Clayton Powell Jr. I studied at Union Theological Seminary in New York City where my academic adviser was James Cone who was just developing the concept of a black theology. When I came to Cleveland in 1987, I met and became a friend and confidant of Carl Stokes, the first black mayor of any major city in America. I also became chairman of the board of the Karamu House Performing Arts Theatre where so much of the artistic heritage of African Americans had been shaped since its founding in 1917. In short, I acknowledge the fact that I am the beneficiary of good locations from which to observe African American life.

I acknowledge the love and patience of my darling wife, Peggy, whose gracious, Georgia-born manner has blessed my life since we were married in 1975. I also acknowledge my son, Aaron, who has contributed to this book by writing the entry on hip-hop culture. I can handle Motown and Louis Armstrong, but I needed his expertise to grasp the meaning of the music of his generation.

Finally, I express my continuing appreciation to the editorial staff at Judson Press. Randy Frame helped me give shape to this project, and Rebecca Irwin-Diehl has been my adviser and editor as the book has become a reality. She was patient as I pushed the deadline as far back as possible, and she was also gracious as I pleaded for the inclusion of more entries even beyond the time when the manuscript was turned in. Judson Press published my earlier work, *An Encyclopedia of African American Christian Heritage*. I am grateful to them for allowing me to produce this book that pushes the focus of study beyond the topic of religion and allows African American history to be viewed more broadly.

# Section 1
## In the Beginning (1600–1800)

### African Beginnings in America

The first Africans were "imported" to British North America in 1619. That's when twenty black people arrived in Jamestown, Virginia, on a slave ship. These Africans didn't start out as slaves. They were brought over as *indentured servants*, just as many European whites were.

However, by the mid-1660s, Virginia and Maryland began adopting laws that changed the status of all black people living in those colonies. They may have started out as indentured servants, but from now on, the laws declared, they were *slaves*, forced into lifelong servitude.

That was bad enough, but these laws, so-called Black Codes, changed the status of black children. English law had always said that a child's status was decided by his or her father—if Dad was free, the child was free too. But in the colonies, many white men were engaging in sexual relationships with their African servants. So the Black Codes said children would now be in the same class as their mother. If Mom was a slave, so were her kids.

By the eighteenth century, these Black Codes had spread throughout British North America. If you inherited black skin, then you also inherited slavery. The system of legalized enslavement of people of African descent was officially the law of the land in North America.

## The 411 on Benjamin Banneker
### Astronomer, Mathematician, Surveyor

■ Born free on November 9, 1731, in Ellicott Mills, Maryland
■ In 1761, invented the first home-made clock in America—which kept perfect time for more than twenty years
■ In 1789, accurately predicted a solar eclipse
■ In a letter dated August 19, 1791, challenged Secretary of State Thomas Jefferson to abolish slavery—and to start with his own slaves
■ From 1792 to 1802, published an annual almanac for farmers and sent it to Jefferson as proof that blacks were the intellectual equals of whites
■ Died in October 1806
■ Most famous for becoming in 1791 the first black person in the new United States of America to hold a presidential appointment—from George Washington to help survey and plan the nation's capital

## SLAVES HEAR THE GOOD NEWS

The first attempt to share the Christian faith with slaves in North America happened in 1701. That's when the Church of England established a missionary group called the Society for the Propagation of the Gospel in Foreign Parts. The society wanted to minister to the white colonists in North American and to teach Christianity to the slaves and American Indians. The missionaries didn't get far for three main reasons: (1) many slaves were Muslim or followed a native religion and resisted conversion, (2) many of the Africans didn't speak English very well, and (3) most slave owners weren't crazy about teaching their slaves about a faith that celebrated freedom from sin or anything else!

The far more successful effort at spreading the gospel among the slaves happened during the Great Awakening, a time of religious revival which started in the Southern colonies in 1740. Traveling preachers such as George Whitefield and John Wesley attracted large crowds who responded eagerly during their exciting revival services.

## "WE'RE IN THE ARMY NOW"
### Blacks in the American Revolution

**Prince Hall** was born in 1753 in Barbados, West Indies. Migrated to Boston, Massachusetts, in 1765. Protested George Washington's decision to exclude blacks from enlisting in the Continental army. When Hall's protest was upheld, he joined the Massachusetts militia— and opened the door for thousands of black men to fight in the American War of Independence.

### More about Prince Hall

With fourteen other men in 1775, Hall founded the first black Masonic lodge, African Lodge No. 459 of Free and Accepted Masons. By 1798, he established three more black lodges, including the famous Philadelphia lodge, headed by Absalom Jones and Richard Allen (see pages 5 and 7).

**Crispus Attucks** was born in 1723 into slavery in Framingham, Massachusetts, to an African-born father and Native American mother. Escaped slavery and worked on a whaling ship in Boston Harbor (of "Boston Tea Party" fame). Joined the patriot cause and was the first person killed in the Boston Massacre on March 5, 1770. A monument in his memory still stands on the Boston Commons.

**Lemuel Haynes** was born into slavery in 1753 to a white mother and black father in West Hartford, Connecticut. Abandoned by his mother and raised as an infant by the

---

**indentured servant:** a person who worked without pay for a set period of time—usually seven years—often to pay back a debt, such as the cost of passage on a ship from Europe to the British colonies in North America.

**slave:** a person who worked without pay for life—or until obtaining freedom through purchase, escape, or emancipation by a liberal owner. Slaves were considered the property of their "employers."

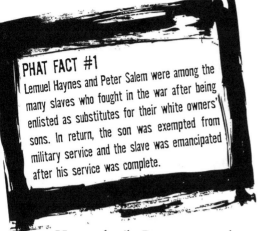

PHAT FACT #1
Lemuel Haynes and Peter Salem were among the many slaves who fought in the war after being enlisted as substitutes for their white owners' sons. In return, the son was exempted from military service and the slave was emancipated after his service was complete.

Haynes family. Became a member of the Massachusetts militia (the "minutemen") in 1774 and fought in the famous battle of Lexington and Concord on April 19, 1775. He was later emancipated and became a minister in the Congregational Church.

### More about Lemuel Haynes

In 1804, Haynes moved to Vermont to work among the poor there. As a result, he became the first black person to receive an honorary degree from Middlebury College in Vermont.

**Peter Salem** was born in 1750 into slavery in Framingham, Massachusetts, and fought at the battle of Lexington and Concord. Because he fought as a stand-in for the son of his white owner, Salem was emancipated after that battle and went on to earn distinction in the battle of Bunker Hill on June 17, 1775, when he reportedly killed a British officer, Major John Pitcairn.

**Salem Poor** was born in 1750 into slavery in Massachusetts but purchased his freedom at age nineteen for the equivalent of an average man's yearly salary. Joined the minutemen in 1775 and fought first at the battle of Bunker Hill and then later in the Continental army under General George Washington at Valley Forge, Saratoga, and Monmouth.

### More about Salem Poor

In a petition dated December 5, 1775, fourteen officers wrote to the General Court of Massachusetts recommending a monetary gift for Poor's heroism under fire, saying, "It would be tedious to go into detail regarding his heroic conduct. We only beg leave to say, in the person of this said Negro centers a brave and gallant soldier." The court never acted on the petition.

### "THIS FAR BY FAITH" Firsts in African American Christian History

**George Liele** was born in slavery in 1773. This pioneer preacher established the first known black congregation in North

America, a Baptist church on his owner's property in Silver Bluff, South Carolina. Later Liele was freed to devote himself to itinerant (traveling) ministry.

**Andrew Bryan** was born in 1737 in slavery in Goose Creek, South Carolina, and a convert of Liele, Bryan became one of the first black Americans to be ordained to the ministry. Organized the First, Second, and Third African Baptist Churches of Savannah, Georgia, despite resistance from whites and even frequent public whippings.

**John Chavis** was born free in 1763 in Granville, North Carolina, Chavis enjoyed a privileged education as a private student of the president of the College of New Jersey (now Princeton University). He was licensed as a Presbyterian preacher to serve as a riding missionary to free blacks and slaves.
▶▶**Fast Forward to the 1800s:**
**JOHN CHAVIS**
From 1801 to 1831, part of Chavis's ministry involved being headmaster of four preparatory schools, which taught the same classic curriculum (including Greek and Latin!) to white students during the day and black students at night. These highly regarded schools thrived during this time. After thirty years, the schools were forced to close after the Nat Turner slave uprising in Virginia (see page 25). Angry and fearful whites in the slave states outlawed free blacks (such as Chavis) from preaching to slaves and restricted the education of free blacks as well as slaves. Chavis kept working as a preacher and teacher until his death in 1838. By 1850, in the areas where his schools had been, more than 40 percent of free black adults had become literate.

**Absalom Jones** was born in 1746 into slavery in Sussex County, Delaware. Jones purchased freedom for himself and his wife and moved to Philadelphia. He helped organize the all-black St. Thomas Episcopal Church there in 1794, and in 1795 he became the first black Episcopal priest.

**Richard Allen** was born in 1760 into slavery in Philadelphia. Allen eventually earned his own freedom in 1786. He organized the all-black congregation of Bethel African Church in 1799.
▶▶**Fast Forward to the 1800s:**
**RICHARD ALLEN**
Allen's African Methodist Episcopal Church—the first black

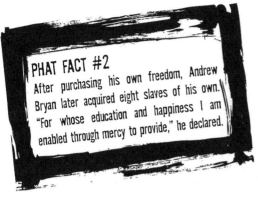

PHAT FACT #2
After purchasing his own freedom, Andrew Bryan later acquired eight slaves of his own. "For whose education and happiness I am enabled through mercy to provide," he declared.

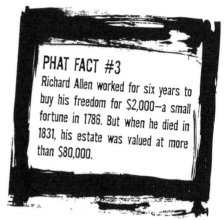

PHAT FACT #3
Richard Allen worked for six years to buy his freedom for $2,000—a small fortune in 1786. But when he died in 1831, his estate was valued at more than $80,000.

denomination—was established in 1816. Also during that year he became their first bishop. James Varick's group (see entry below) was organized in 1822 under the name "African Methodist Episcopal Church of New York City," and Varick became their first bishop that same year. (Zion wasn't added to the official name until 1848.) At that time, the two new black denominations discussed and rejected an affiliation. But they agreed to expand in different directions. Varick and his group would focus on New York and the rest of New England. Allen and followers would concentrate on Pennsylvania, Maryland, Delaware, and New Jersey.

## The Free African Society

**WHAT?** First black-founded financial institution in America
**WHEN?** May 1787
**BY WHOM?** Richard Allen and Absalom Jones
**WHERE?** Philadelphia, Pennsylvania
**WHY?** To provide financial services (like a modern credit union), moral guidance, and assistance with funeral costs to free blacks

**James Varick** was born in 1750 in Newburgh, New York. Varick is believed to have had little education but became a teacher and shoemaker. In 1796 he led a group of black members out of New York City's John Street Methodist Episcopal Church to protest discrimination they experienced there. He later formed an independent church that eventually evolved into the African Methodist Episcopal Zion Church.

## The 411 on Richard Allen

■ Born a slave on February 14, 1760, in Philadelphia, Pennsylvania
■ Purchased his freedom in 1786
■ In 1787, with Absalom Jones, organized the Free African Society, a mutual aid society for free blacks in Philadelphia
■ Refused opportunity to travel with famous Methodist evangelist Bishop Francis Asbury because it meant pretending to be Asbury's slave when traveling through slaveholding regions of the country
■ In November 1787, led walkout of blacks from St. George Methodist Episcopal Church in response to segregated seating policy
■ Organized Bethel African Church, an all-black congregation, which was dedicated by Bishop Asbury in April 1799
■ On April 11, 1816, was consecrated first bishop of the first black denomination, the African Methodist Episcopal Church
■ Owned several businesses in Philadelphia, including a blacksmith shop, shoemaking factory, and chimney sweep company
■ Best known for his belief in an all-black church, for his outspoken opposition to slavery, and for his entrepreneurial commitment to hard work and thrift

**"ORDE OUR STEPS"**
**Landmark Events in Black History**

Richard Allen nurtured a sizable black membership at St. George Methodist Episcopal Church in Philadelphia—so sizable that the whites who came to worship had trouble finding seats. The church leadership established a seating policy that relegated blacks to standing room on the first floor

**PHAT FACT #4**
In 1770, at age 17, Phillis Wheatley became the first African American to publish a poem (about the death of revivalist George Whitefield.) In 1773, her collected poems became the first book published by an African American woman.

## The Stono Rebellion

**WHEN?** September 9, 1739
**WHERE?** Near Charleston, South Carolina
**WHO?** Almost 100 slaves, the largest uprising in history to date
**WHY?** Probably the soon-to-be-enacted Security Act, which required white men to carry firearms to church on Sunday—the only day many slaves could work for themselves. That meant they could travel more freely—without harassment or suspicion—on that day.
**WHAT HAPPENED?** Twenty slaves, men and women, gathered at a gun shop near the Stono River. With guns obtained from the shop, the slaves killed the two shopkeepers and marched south (probably toward Florida and Spanish freedom) under banners proclaiming "Liberty." They went from house to house, killing whatever whites they met, with other slaves joining them along the way. Late in the afternoon, after marching ten miles and killing between twenty and twenty-five whites, the slaves met a group of heavily armed whites. The slaves shot first—but in the first volley of gunfire, the better-armed whites killed fourteen blacks. By nightfall, thirty slaves were dead and thirty had escaped—many of whom were captured and executed over the next six months.
**RESULTS?** The slave states passed new, stricter Black Codes, prohibiting slaves from growing their own food, earning their own money, assembling in groups on their own (without whites), or learning to read and write.

## Did you know...?

The founder of the modern city of Chicago was a man of African descent? Jean Baptiste Pointe du Sable was born on the island we now call Haiti in 1745 to an African mother (slave) and a French father (free). Educated in France, du Sable established a thriving trading post in 1788 on the site where Chicago skyscrapers now rise. His name is remembered with a plaque in the middle of the city's business district and with a high school on the city's south side.

*"And why should it be thought impossible, heterodox, or improper for a woman to preach, seeing the Savior died for the woman as well as the man?"*
—Jarena Lee, evangelist and preacher

and seating in a separate balcony for their exclusive use. Allen suggested constructing a separate building for the rapidly growing black congregation, but the white leaders of the church rejected that idea.

The issue became critical in November 1787. Several black members of the church were on the way to the "reserved" section when the congregation was called to prayer. Rather than disturb the service by continuing to walk, the black members knelt to join in the prayer—in the whites-only section of the building. The ushers attempted to force them to rise and move, so when the prayer ended, instead of continuing on to the black section of the sanctuary, the black worshipers walked out of that church as a protest of the practice of segregation in the church. Richard Allen and Absalom Jones were among those who led the walkout that day.

Jones didn't share Allen's belief in an all-black church; he felt the church shouldn't be segregated. So Jones and Allen went their own ways. Jones became the first black man ordained as a priest in the Episcopal Church in 1794. In contrast, Allen organized the all-black Bethel African Church in Philadelphia, almost twenty years after the walkout at St. George's. Allen saw his dream of an all-black church fulfilled—in April 1816 he became bishop of the African Methodist Episcopal Church. That first black denomination was a conglomerate of similarly minded congregations from Maryland, Delaware, and New Jersey. They all had rejected the racial segregation common in churches in their area.

### ▶▶Fast Forward to 2000: VASHTI MURPHY McKENZIE

In the year 2000, the Rev. Dr. Vashti McKenzie of Baltimore, Maryland, became the first female bishop elected by the African Methodist Episcopal Church.

# Legislating Race in America, 1787

## THE NORTHWEST ORDINANCE

Legislation passed by the Continental Congress that made slavery illegal anywhere in the northwestern territories that later became the states of Ohio, Indiana, Illinois, Michigan, and Wisconsin. The idea was that no new slave states would be added to the growing union.

## UNITED STATES CONSTITUTION

The founding fathers hotly debated key articles of the Constitution of the new United States of America—three of which dealt with the status of blacks in America. Legalized slavery might have died as the United States was born, but in the end, the Constitution was ratified with these three key articles intact:

**Article I, Section 2:** For the purpose of taxation and representation, an indentured servant was counted as a full citizen, but a slave (i.e., a person of African descent) was counted as 3/5 of a person.

**Article I, Section 9:** The most hotly debated article, this section allowed the continuation of the trans-African slave trade until 1808. After that time, the sale and purchase of U.S.–born slaves was allowed, but it was illegal to import new slaves from outside the United States.

**Article IV, Section 2:** No slave was permitted to escape slavery by fleeing a slave state and seeking freedom elsewhere; the law required citizens to return the escaped slave to his or her owner.

## PHAT FACT #4

Jarena Lee was the first black woman recognized as a preacher in the United States. Born free in 1783, she was a member of Bethel African Church in Philadelphia. Her pastor, Richard Allen, acknowledged her call to ministry, but Lee was never ordained.

# Section 2
## Let My People Go! (1800–1861)

### The Battle over Slavery

During the years leading up to the Civil War, the country was divided between those who were for slavery and those who were against it. Needless to say, black Americans—both slave and free—wanted to see an end to this inhumane way of life. And there were some white Americans who thought that having slaves was wrong. In fact, the whole antislavery, or *abolitionist*, movement had both black and white members.

But the question wasn't just about whether slavery was good or bad. The South needed slaves as a form of cheap labor to help landowners make their profits. The North, which was becoming more industrialized, had a steady stream of *immigrants* coming to America from Europe who could be paid low wages and didn't have to be "owned." So there was a conflict between slave labor and "free" labor.

Then there were arguments over whether the South had the right to decide for itself if it would have slavery without the federal government telling it what to do, and whether slavery would be allowed in the new western territories.

But there were tensions even among blacks: some looked for a peaceful way to end slavery while others were ready to take part in *insurrections*. Some blacks wanted to stay in America and work to make it a better place to live. Others wanted to *emigrate* back to Africa and start a new life in their native land.

These divisions—between North and South, slave and free, black and white, even white versus white and black versus black—drew our country into one of the most troubled times in its history. It eventually led to the start of the Civil War in 1861.

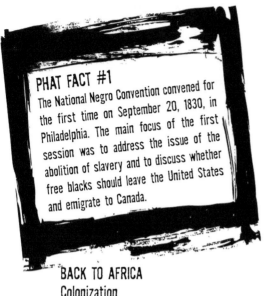

## BACK TO AFRICA
### Colonization

The movement to resettle free-born blacks and emancipated slaves from America to communities outside of the United States—mostly in Africa, Canada, and Haiti—was known as colonization. This hotly debated movement was largely opposed by black leaders who viewed America as their native land. They didn't like the idea that whites could forcibly bring blacks from Africa over to America to labor as slaves and then remove these same black people from the country they had helped to build. But there were many black religious leaders—such as Henry Highland Garnet, Lott Carey, and Martin Delany—who actively supported the idea of emigration.

The issue of colonization was also linked to the cause of *Christianization*. This was the idea that free blacks who were willing

---

**abolitionist**: a person who believed that owning slaves was morally wrong and demanded an end to the institution of slavery in the United States

**colonization**: to settle by force a group of people in a new area or region of another country

**emancipate**: to free or release from slavery

**emigrate**: to leave one's country to live in another country

**immigrant**: a person who has come to another country in search of opportunities or safety

**insurrection**: to revolt or plan a revolt against a country or government authority

**Underground Railroad**: a secret network of escape routes and safe houses known as "stations"—led by free blacks, former slaves, and sympathetic whites known as "conductors"—that helped thousands of slaves escape to freedom

## The American Colonization Society

**WHAT?** An organization founded to resettle free blacks and emancipated slaves in West Africa
**WHEN?** Founded in 1816–17
**BY WHOM?** Rev. Robert Finley, a Presbyterian minister, who rallied federal officials as well as Northern abolitionists, Southern slaveholders, and church groups
**WHERE?** The group purchased land in what is now known as the African country of Liberia.
**WHY?** There were many reasons: (1) Some blacks thought Africa offered a better life. (2) Some whites opposed slavery but didn't want integration. (3) Slave owners didn't want their slaves mixing with free blacks. (4) Some wanted to spread Christianity in the new colony. (5) Some hoped a free Liberian cotton industry would offer an alternative to U.S. slave labor in European markets.
**RESULT?** Disputes between members, lack of funding, and lack of public support—especially from blacks—doomed the group. Over several decades, they settled only a few thousand blacks in West Africa.

to resettle in Africa would be able to share the Christian faith with the African people.

### MORE SUPPORTERS OF EMIGRATION

**Martin Delany** was born on May 6, 1812, in Charles Town, Virginia, to a slave father and a free black mother. In 1822 his mother took Martin and his siblings and fled to Pennsylvania rather than face imprisonment for learning how to read, a crime for black people in Virginia at that time. Delany studied at the African Methodist Episcopal night school in Pittsburgh and was accepted into Harvard Medical School in 1851. However, he was expelled from Harvard after white students protested his presence at the school.

In 1852 Delany published a booklet titled *The Condition, Elevation, Emigration and Destiny of the Colored People of the United States*, and he hosted a National Emigration Convention in Cleveland, Ohio, in 1854. He went to what is now Nigeria and established a settlement in 1858. He returned to the United States to recruit more black emigrants for his new colony, but he met with little success. The outbreak of the Civil War disrupted Delany's plans, and he became a recruiter for

## The 411 on Henry Highland Garnet

- Born into slavery on December 23, 1815, in Maryland
- Escaped with his family to New York City in 1825
- Became a Presbyterian minister and served the Liberty Street Negro Presbyterian Church in the town of Troy, New York
- Turned the church into a station for the Underground Railroad
- Was active with the American Anti-Slavery Society
- Emigrated to England where he worked with antislavery groups urging English companies to stop buying cotton and other goods made by slave labor
- Returned to the United States in 1856 and pastored Shiloh Presbyterian Church of New York City
- Founded the African Civilization Society in 1858 to help free blacks emigrate to Liberia and Sierra Leone
- Appointed general consul to Liberia in 1881

all black regiments that would fight in the Union (Northern) army.

**Lott Carey** was born in 1780 into slavery in Charles City, Virginia. He converted to Christianity in 1807 and was licensed by the First Baptist Church of Richmond to be a preacher. He purchased his freedom in 1813 for $850, which was enough not only for himself but for his wife and their three children as well.

In 1815, Carey helped to start the Richmond African Baptist Missionary Society, and he began to raise the funds needed for his mission to a suitable location in Africa. He and a group of free blacks set sail from Richmond for Sierra Leone in West Africa on January 23, 1821. They arrived in early March of that

**PHAT FACT #2**
After relocating to Liberia in 1822, Lott Carey became governor of that colony in 1828.

year, and by 1822 they had relocated and established a settlement in Liberia.

Carey wanted to make a mission trip to Africa for two reasons: (1) missionary zeal caused him to want to share the gospel with people in Africa who had never heard the story of Jesus, and (2) he believed that his own best chance of developing as a man was to be found outside of the United States. He believed that the reality of slavery and the prejudices displayed even toward free blacks would prevent him from reaching his fullest potential. In words that would mirror the language of Martin Luther King Jr.

more than a hundred years later, he said he wanted "to go to a country where I shall be estimated by my merits, not by my complexion."

## THE ABOLITIONIST MOVEMENT

The abolitionist movement in the United States emerged as early as 1770 as an organized protest to the continued presence of slavery. The local antislavery societies located in many Northern states were strengthened by the formation of the American Anti-Slavery Society in 1833, which brought unity and focus to the abolitionist

**PHAT FACT #3**
Martin Delany was commissioned during the Civil War to serve in the Union army with a rank of major. He became the first black person to serve as a field officer in the American military.

## Did you know...?

President Abraham Lincoln proposed a colonization plan for free and emancipated blacks living in the United States. His plan was to resettle blacks on the island of Vache off the coast of Haiti. In 1863, an initial group of five hundred colonists was sent to the island. However, two hundred died from tropical diseases and other hardships within months of arriving. The survivors were picked up and returned to the United States, and the project was abandoned.

## The 411 on William Lloyd Garrison

■ Born into a poor family in Newburyport, Massachusetts, on December 10, 1805

■ Moved to Boston in 1828 to work for a newspaper there and met antislavery leader Benjamin Lundy

■ Worked as coeditor of Lundy's abolitionist newspaper until dismissed over the fiery content of several of his antislavery columns

■ First issue of his newspaper, the *Liberator*, appeared on the streets of Boston on January 1, 1831.

■ In 1833, helped found the American Anti-Slavery Society

■ Once embraced the idea of black emigration but later became an outspoken critic of the American Colonization Society

■ Resigned from the American Anti-Slavery Society over his belief that voting rights should not be a part of the abolitionist agenda

movement. In addition to sympathetic whites such as William Lloyd Garrison and Wendell Phillips, many notable black religious leaders, including James Pennington, Sojourner Truth, Samuel Cornish, Samuel Ringgold Ward, Alexander Crummell, Peter Williams Jr., and Henry Highland Garnet, were also active in that abolitionist organization.

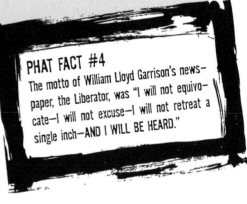

PHAT FACT #4

The motto of William Lloyd Garrison's newspaper, the Liberator, was "I will not equivocate—I will not excuse—I will not retreat a single inch—AND I WILL BE HEARD."

## Did you know...?

Because Frederick Douglass's speeches were widely advertised, making his whereabouts a matter of common knowledge, friends within the antislavery community in England purchased his freedom for 150 pounds sterling, allowing him to travel freely without fear of being captured and returned to slavery.

More about Frederick Douglass and William Lloyd Garrison

The two men strongly disagreed on the use of violence as a means toward ending slavery. Douglass believed that the "cartridge box" was an essential tool in the battle against slavery. Garrison, on the other hand, did not embrace violence as the means by which to achieve the abolitionists' goal.

▶▶Fast Forward
to the Post-Civil War Years:
FREDERICK DOUGLASS
After the Civil War, Frederick Douglass became active in the Republican Party. His loyalty was rewarded with a series of government appointments.

Also, by the 1880s, his focus had expanded from the issue of rights for blacks to include the issue of women's suffrage (right to vote).

## MORE ABOLITIONISTS

**James W. C. Pennington** was born into slavery in 1809. He was trained to be a blacksmith but ran away from slavery and settled in Hartford, Connecticut. By 1841, he had become a leader in the

## The 411 on Frederick Douglass

- Born into slavery near Maryland's eastern shore in 1818
- Taught to read by owner's wife
- While assigned to work in Baltimore, met and married a free woman, Anna Murray, who urged him to run away so they both could be free
- On September 3, 1838, escaped to New York City by posing as a free sailor
- Moved to New Bedford, Massachusetts, and began a twenty-year career as one of the country's most outspoken critics of slavery
- On August 12, 1841, at the invitation of William Lloyd Garrison, delivered his first antislavery speech at an abolitionist rally in Nantucket, Rhode Island
- Active member of the American Anti-Slavery Society
- Began publishing *The North Star* on December 3, 1847

**PHAT FACT #6**
Frederick Douglass did not support some of his contemporaries in their appeals to slaves to rise up and win their freedom by force of arms. He also refused to support John Brown in his 1859 raid on Harper's Ferry.

abolitionist movement. In 1843 and again in 1851, he traveled to London as a delegate from the Connecticut Anti-Slavery Society to the convention of the World Anti-Slavery Society.

He was a close associate of Frederick Douglass and William Lloyd Garrison and contributed to various abolitionist journals.

## The 411 on Sojourner Truth

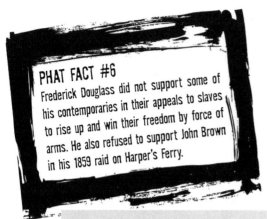

- Born in 1797 into slavery in Ulster County, New York
- Slave name *Isabella*
- Ran away one year before slavery officially ended in the state of New York (in 1827) when her owner broke his promise to free her and her children—just three years before emancipation
- Protected by Quaker family who purchased her freedom; took their family name, becoming Isabella Van Wagener
- Sued her former owner who had retaliated by illegally selling one of her children across state lines into the slave state of Alabama—and won
- Lifelong member of the African Methodist Episcopal Zion Church
- In 1843, called by God in a vision to be an itinerant preacher—and to change her name to fit the task: Sojourner Truth
- Became a leading abolitionist and advocate for women's rights
- Famous for her 1851 "Ain't I a woman?" speech for women's rights, delivered in Akron, Ohio, in defense of her rights as a black woman
- Recruited black Union soldiers for Massachusetts and Maryland militia during the Civil War
- Was granted a private audience with President Abraham Lincoln in October 1864

## Did you know...?

Ninety years before Rosa Parks refused to give up her bus seat to a white man in Montgomery, Alabama, Sojourner Truth refused to sit down in the "colored section" of a Washington, D.C., streetcar in 1865. A conductor threw her from the car, badly injuring her. But as a result, the segregation policy was suspended.

On November 5, 1859, the *Weekly Anglo-American* ran his article titled "Pray for John Brown." It was a call for support for John Brown after his arrest and trial following the raid at Harpers Ferry, Virginia.

Pennington opposed the American Colonization Society, but he was a supporter of the idea of spreading the gospel among the people of Africa.

**Wendell Phillips** was born to a wealthy family in Boston and attended Harvard University and Harvard Law School. He was on his way to a life of privilege and comfort until he came upon a mob that was dragging William Lloyd Garrison through the streets of Boston with a rope tied around his neck. Witnessing that event—along with marrying a woman who said she would wed him only if he shared her abolitionist beliefs—changed the course of his life.

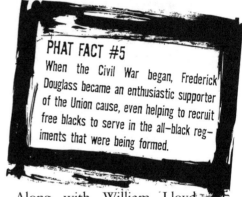

PHAT FACT #5
When the Civil War began, Frederick Douglass became an enthusiastic supporter of the Union cause, even helping to recruit free blacks to serve in the all-black regiments that were being formed.

Along with William Lloyd Garrison, Phillips became a coleader of the American Anti-Slavery Society. However, Phillips did not embrace the passive resistance methods of Garrison. Instead, he embraced the raid of John Brown at Harpers Ferry. Moreover, when the Civil War erupted, he urged that free blacks

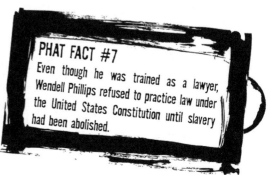

PHAT FACT #7
Even though he was trained as a lawyer, Wendell Phillips refused to practice law under the United States Constitution until slavery had been abolished.

"We wish to plead our own cause. Too long have others spoken for us. Too long has the public been deceived by misrepresentations, in thinking which concerns us dearly. . . . It shall never be our object to court controversy, though we must at all times consider ourselves as champions in defense of oppressed humanity."

—From the mission statement of FREEDOM'S JOURNAL

## More about James W. C. Pennington

In 1855, while challenging the law that prohibited black people from riding on public transportation in New York City, Pennington was thrown off a horse-drawn trolley. He sued the company for injuries sustained and for refusing to grant him equal protection under the law when it came to public transportation. He won the case and opened up access to public transit to all people regardless of race.

## "SPREAD THE WORD!" Famous Publications by Black Abolitionists

☞ *Freedom's Journal* newspaper published by John Russworm and Samuel Cornish, 1827–1829
☞ "David Walker's Appeal to the Colored Citizens of the World but

join the Union army to end slavery by force of arms.

Phillips also disagreed with Garrison on the issue of black voting rights. He believed that blacks should enjoy every right enjoyed by whites, including the right to vote. When Garrison resigned as president of the American Anti-Slavery Society over the issue of voting rights for blacks, Phillips succeeded him as president.

PHAT FACT #8
*Freedom's Journal* went out of business after Cornish and Russworm split over these fundamental issues: Cornish remained committed to the abolitionist goal of gaining full citizenship rights for blacks in America. Russworm embraced emigration with blacks establishing new lives in Africa.

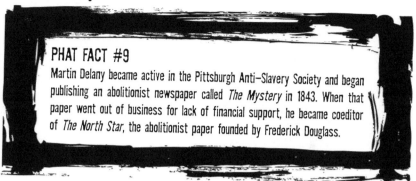

**PHAT FACT #9**

Martin Delany became active in the Pittsburgh Anti-Slavery Society and began publishing an abolitionist newspaper called *The Mystery* in 1843. When that paper went out of business for lack of financial support, he became coeditor of *The North Star*, the abolitionist paper founded by Frederick Douglass.

in Particular…to Those of the United States of America" by David Walker, 1829

✑ Widely circulated antislavery speech delivered on July 4, 1830, by Peter Williams Jr.

✑ "An Address to the Slaves of the United States of America" by Henry Highland Garnet, 1943

✑ *The North Star* newspaper published by Frederick Douglass, first issue 1847

✑ Antislavery speech delivered on July 4, 1852, by Frederick Douglass

**More about the FREEDOM'S JOURNAL**

✑ First newspaper in America to be owned and operated by black African Americans

✑ Began circulating in New York City on March 16, 1827

✑ Founded and edited by Samuel Cornish and John Russworm

✑ One of the few newspapers in the country that reported positively on life in the nation's black communities

✑ Argued in editorials for the abolition of slavery

✑ Published before William Garrison's *The Liberator* and Frederick Douglass's *The North Star*

▶▶**Fast Forward to 1872:**

**WILLIAM STILL**

A stationmaster for the Underground Railroad in Philadelphia and a leader in the Philadelphia Anti-Slavery Society, William Still published his book *The Underground Railroad* in 1872. The book documents many of the people and events that made up the network. Still's book recounts the dangers faced by more than eight hundred slaves who escaped with his assistance.

**LEGISLATING RACE IN AMERICA**
**The Fugitive Slave Act of 1850**

The Fugitive Slave Act was enacted in response to the number of slaves who were running away in search of freedom. This law was a much

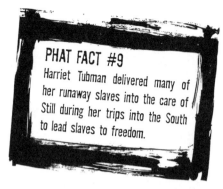

**PHAT FACT #9**
Harriet Tubman delivered many of her runaway slaves into the care of Still during her trips into the South to lead slaves to freedom.

## Did you know...?

Harriet Tubman always began her escapes on a Saturday night, knowing that a runaway slave could not be reported until the start of working hours the next Monday. That gave her a 24-hour headstart on slave catchers.

tougher version of the Fugitive Slave Act passed by Congress in 1793. This new law included three controversial parts that served to widen the gap between the North and the South and to push the United States closer to the Civil War.

**1.** If a runaway slave was tracked down by a bounty hunter or by the "rightful owner," no jury trial was required to make certain

that the person being captured and returned to slavery was the actual runaway in question. So the person who had escaped from slavery couldn't bring a legal action to argue for the right to stay where he or she was living. Worse yet, the person could not sue to prove that he or she was not the person who was being sought.

**2.** A law enforcement official who knew where a runaway slave was but refused to cooperate with a slave owner to get that person back could be fined $1,000. A private citizen who knew that an owner was looking for a runaway slave but who still provided shelter or help to that person could be fined $2,000.

**3.** Special commissioners decided whether the identity of a runaway slave had been established.

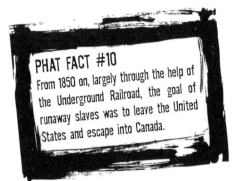

**PHAT FACT #10**
From 1850 on, largely through the help of the Underground Railroad, the goal of runaway slaves was to leave the United States and escape into Canada.

Frederick Douglass once said that the best response to the Fugitive Slave Act was "a good revolver, a steady hand, and a determination to shoot down any man attempting to kidnap a fugitive slave."

All that was needed was the sworn affidavit of the slave owner claiming that the runaway slave had been captured.

When a runaway slave could not be found, it was not unheard of for bounty hunters and slave owners to simply kidnap free black people off the streets of Northern cities and force them into slavery.

As a result of the Fugitive Slave Act, runaway slaves weren't safe from being recaptured anywhere in the United States, even in

"There was one of two things I had a right to, liberty or death; if I could not have one, I would have the other, for no man should take me alive."

—Harriet Tubman, "conductor" on the Underground Railroad

## The 411 on Harriet Tubman

- Born in 1820 into slavery in Bucktown, Maryland
- At age twelve, hit in forehead with a two-pound weight by a white overseer trying to discipline a runaway slave; injury caused her to fall asleep without warning, sometimes two or three times a day, for the rest of her life
- Escaped from slavery in 1849 when she learned that her master was going to sell her to pay off some of his debts
- Made her way to Philadelphia traveling alone and always at night, using roads, tunnels, and safe houses of the Underground Railroad
- As a "conductor" on the Underground Railroad, traveled to Maryland or Delaware twice a year for the next ten years to lead slaves to freedom
- Carried on each trip a pistol, ammunition, forged slave passes, a tonic that would put crying babies to sleep, and a small amount of money
- Made a total of nineteen trips and helped more than three hundred people escape slavery

## Did you know...?

When Wilberforce University was established in 1856 by the African Methodist Episcopal Church in Wilberforce, Ohio, it was the first university organized by blacks in the history of the United States.

states where slavery had already been abolished.

### More about Harriet Tubman

On June 2, 1863, Harriet Tubman led three hundred black soldiers on a raid on a part of South Carolina still under control of the Confederate army. During that raid, the black Union soldiers with her burned several warehouses full of Confederate food and supplies worth millions of dollars. The raid also resulted in the liberation of more than seven hundred slaves.

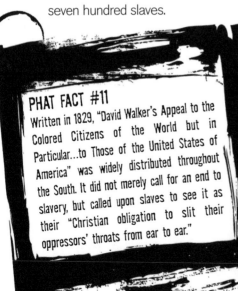

**PHAT FACT #11**

Written in 1829, "David Walker's Appeal to the Colored Citizens of the World but in Particular...to Those of the United States of America" was widely distributed throughout the South. It did not merely call for an end to slavery, but called upon slaves to see it as their "Christian obligation to slit their oppressors' throats from ear to ear."

▶▶**Fast Forward**
**to 1900: HARRIET TUBMAN**
Before her death in 1913, Harriet Tubman was active in the women's suffrage (right to vote) movement with Susan B. Anthony. She also used her celebrity status to raise money for a old-age home for impoverished elderly black people.

## A FORCE TO BE RECKONED WITH
### Insurrection!

Born into slavery around 1775, Gabriel Prosser recruited more than a thousand slaves to take part in an insurrection planned for August 30, 1800, in Richmond, Virginia. The plan was to kill all the white people in Richmond, with the exception of the whites who had been sympathetic to the antislavery cause (the Quakers, the Methodists, and the French).

On the day of the attack, the slaves gathered six miles outside of the city armed with a few guns and homemade bayonets, scythes, and clubs. However, a violent rain storm erupted and prevented the revolt from taking place. But even before that, some white residents had gotten suspicious and called out the state militia. The uprising was no longer possible, and most of the slaves returned to their respective farms and homes.

However, thirty-five people, including Prosser, were eventually executed for planning what would have one of been the largest slave insurrection ever conducted in the United States.

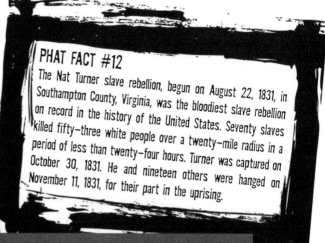

**PHAT FACT #12**

The Nat Turner slave rebellion, begun on August 22, 1831, in Southampton County, Virginia, was the bloodiest slave rebellion on record in the history of the United States. Seventy slaves killed fifty-three white people over a twenty-mile radius in a period of less than twenty-four hours. Turner was captured on October 30, 1831. He and nineteen others were hanged on November 11, 1831, for their part in the uprising.

## The Denmark Vesey Uprising

**WHEN?** Initial date: July 14, 1822, which was moved back by Vesey to June 16, 1822

**WHERE?** South Carolina

**WHO?** Eight thousand slaves

**WHY?** While still a slave, Vesey saw the brutality of slavery while working on his owner's slave ship. After purchasing his freedom, he wanted to use his liberty to help secure the freedom of other slaves and to end the slave system once and for all.

**WHAT WAS THE PLAN?** The plan was for eight thousand slaves equipped with bayonets and daggers to kill every white person they encountered and thereby end slavery first in Charleston. They would move from plantation to plantation until all the whites had been killed and all the slaves had been liberated. They would then move to other states and do the same thing until slavery was eradicated by force of arms and bloodshed.

**WHAT WENT WRONG?** Word of the planned uprising was leaked to a house slave who in turn reported the plan to the son of his owner. The plan unraveled as more blacks were arrested and questioned. Vesey called off the uprising on June 10, but it had already been revealed that he was the leader of the planned insurrection.

**RESULTS?** Vesey and sixty-six others were convicted and hung. As a result of the planned uprising, whites in South Carolina enacted a sweeping number of changes that made any future attempt at planning a coordinated attack such as the one planned by Vesey virtually impossible.

### The Amistad Revolt

The *Amistad* Revolt took place on 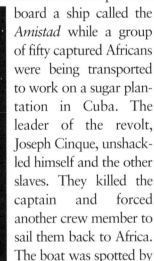 board a ship called the *Amistad* while a group of fifty captured Africans were being transported to work on a sugar plantation in Cuba. The leader of the revolt, Joseph Cinque, unshackled himself and the other slaves. They killed the captain and forced another crew member to sail them back to Africa. The boat was spotted by a United States Navy vessel and taken into custody. The Africans were charged with murder.

The first trial found that the people on the *Amistad* should be allowed to return to Africa. The case was argued all the way to the U.S. Supreme Court, which upheld the trial court's ruling. Funds were raised, and thirty of the original persons on the *Amistad* were returned to Sierra Leone in mid-January 1842.

### IN SEARCH OF JUSTICE
### The Dred
### Scott Decision

■ Dred Scott was born into slavery in Virginia in 1800.

■ In 1833, Scott and his family were slaves belonging to Dr. John Emerson, an army doctor.

■ Emerson took Scott and his family on tours of duty to live in non-slave-holding states where they lived for several years.

■ Abolitionists started a lawsuit on behalf of Dred Scott, arguing that he should be set free from slavery because he had become a free person by living in free states for most of ten years.

■ The case made it to the United States Supreme Court.

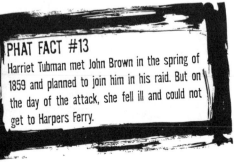

**PHAT FACT #13**
Harriet Tubman met John Brown in the spring of 1859 and planned to join him in his raid. But on the day of the attack, she fell ill and could not get to Harpers Ferry.

**PHAT FACT #14**
The Civil War broke out in 1861—four years after the Dred Scott Decision.

■ In 1857, the Supreme Court ruled that blacks were not citizens and therefore could not sue in the courts to solve their problems.

■ The Supreme Court also declared as unconstitutional the Missouri Compromise of 1820, which had established limits on where slavery could be expanded as new states joined the Union.

## More about the Dred Scott Decision

The Dred Scott ruling fueled anti-slavery sentiments throughout the North and sharpened the issue of slavery as one that had the potential to permanently divide the nation.

## John Brown's Raid

**WHEN?** October 16, 1859
**WHERE?** Harpers Ferry, Virginia
**WHO?** John Brown, five blacks, and sixteen whites, including two of Brown's sons
**WHY?** Brown was angered by the passage of the 1850 Fugitive Slave Act. The next event that pushed him into action was the spread of slavery into the western territories.
**WHAT WAS THE PLAN?** The plan, which Brown began twelve years earlier, involved seizing the weapons in the federal arsenal at Harpers Ferry. The group would also cut the telegraph lines so word of the uprising would not spread. Brown and his group would then wage guerilla war from the Blue Ridge Mountains of Virginia by attacking slave-holders and freeing as many slaves as possible.
**WHAT WENT WRONG?** No slaves or other sympathetic whites joined Brown's raid. Also, an express trained rolled through the town and passengers saw what was happening. Within hours word had spread to Washington, D.C. President Buchanan dispatched a unit of army soldiers. Within thirty-six hours, the plan that John Brown had been developing for twelve years had ended in defeat.
**RESULTS?** One month later, on December 2, 1859, John Brown was hung for his role in leading the raid at Harpers Ferry. But his death did not end the antislavery fervor in the country. It served as an additional spark that helped to ignite the Civil War.

# Section 3
## Free at Last! (1861–1900)

## Civil War, Emancipation, and Reconstruction

The Civil War began in 1861 with the battle of Bull Run and ended in 1865 with the surrender of General Robert E. Lee at Appomattox Court House. Within the space of those four years, armies of the North and the South engaged in fierce battles. Some of the most famous Union victories were the battles of Antietam, Vicksburg, Gettysburg, and Shiloh. Some of the more well-known Confederate victories were won at the first and second battles of Manasseh, the first and second battles of Bull Run, and the battles of Chancellorsville and Fredericksburg.

The loss of life that resulted from four years of war was tremendous. Adding together deaths from both Union and Confederate soldiers, more than six hundred thousand soldiers lost their lives. And most of these deaths were not the result of battlefield wounds but were caused by disease. Basic hygiene was either not known or not easily practiced on the field. Also, there were no vaccinations or immunizations, which we take for granted today. Therefore, the camps where these soldiers lived were breeding grounds for disease.

During the war, the role of blacks within American society began to shift, even if only slightly. The Emancipation Proclamation in 1863 freed the slaves of slaveholding states—but that freedom could only be enjoyed if those slaves came to the North. Also in 1863, the 54th Massachusetts Regiment—the North's first unit of black soldiers—was formed. The bravery of these troops on the battlefield led the way for the creation of more than fifty more regiments of black soldiers.

During the period after the Civil War—known as Reconstruction—the Southern states rejoined the Union. In addition, blacks were given the right to vote and other political freedoms—although these were, for the most part, short-lived. And perhaps most dramatically, with the North's victory over the South with its slaveholding, rural economy, the United States took a giant step forward into the industrial age.

## AFRICAN AMERICANS AND THE MILITARY

The 54th Massachusetts Regiment was formed in 1863 as the first regiment of Northern black soldiers during the Civil War. Black volunteers were recruited from throughout the North to join. From the start, the 54th was seen as a way for black soldiers to prove that they were just as good as any other soldier, if not better.

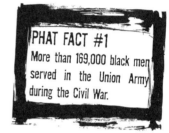

**PHAT FACT #1**
More than 169,000 black men served in the Union Army during the Civil War.

The men got their chance to fight in a major battle on July 18, 1863, when the regiment led the charge against Fort Wagner. They were to be followed by several other white regiments, but the Confederate defense of the fort was so strong that it could not be captured. Of the 600 men in the 54th, 267 were killed or wounded.

### Did you know...?

Sergeant William H. Carney became the first African American to receive the Congressional Medal of Honor (the highest military honor given in the United States) in recognition of bravery displayed at the Fort Wagner battle. He carried the colors (the American flag) for the regiment after the first flag bearer was mortally wounded, and he also led the charge up a steep hill to the top of the heavily guarded fort. He was severely wounded—twice—during that battle.

**PHAT FACT #2**
A total of twenty-three African Americans received the Congressional Medal of Honor for bravery displayed during the Civil War—several decades after the war ended.

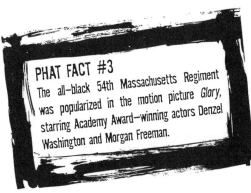

PHAT FACT #3
The all–black 54th Massachusetts Regiment was popularized in the motion picture *Glory*, starring Academy Award–winning actors Denzel Washington and Morgan Freeman.

### Early West Point Graduates

■ Henry O. Flipper, class of 1877, became the first black graduate of the U.S. Military Academy at West Point.

■ In 1887, John Alexander became the second black graduate of West Point.

■ Following Flipper and Alexander, Charles Young—class of

## The 411 on Henry O. Flipper

■ Assigned to the 10th Cavalry, one of the four all-black units that helped in the westward expansion of the United States after the Civil War
■ Served until 1881 when he was involved in a controversial military trial—known as a court martial—that forced him to resign
■ After his court martial, continued to serve the country as a mining engineer and Spanish interpreter

**amendment:** a change or revision
**cavalry:** soldiers trained to fight while riding on horseback
**Confederacy:** the Southern states that separated from the Union
**constitution:** an official document stating a country's rules of law
**infantry:** units of soldiers trained to fight on foot
**jurisdiction:** area of control
**migration:** the movement from one region of a country to another
**proclamation:** a formal announcement, usually made to the public
**ratify:** to approve
**regiment:** a large unit of troops in the military
**secede:** to withdraw or separate
**veto:** to refuse to approve a bill that was passed by the legislature so that it cannot become a law

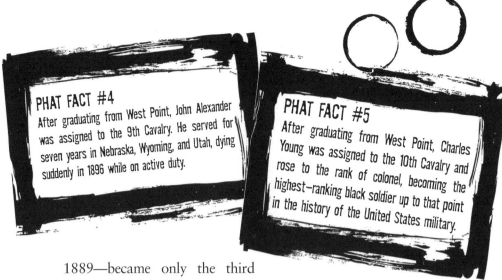

**PHAT FACT #4**
After graduating from West Point, John Alexander was assigned to the 9th Cavalry. He served for seven years in Nebraska, Wyoming, and Utah, dying suddenly in 1896 while on active duty.

**PHAT FACT #5**
After graduating from West Point, Charles Young was assigned to the 10th Cavalry and rose to the rank of colonel, becoming the highest-ranking black soldier up to that point in the history of the United States military.

1889—became only the third black to graduate from West Point.

### Buffalo Soldiers

■ The soldiers of the 9th and 10th Cavalry and the 24th and 25th Infantry were called "buffalo soldiers" by the Native Americans of the Great Plains and the Southwest.

■ They were given that name because their curly black hair and their fierceness in battle reminded the Native Americans of the buffalo that roamed that part of the country.

■ The 9th Cavalry was organized in New Orleans in 1866. They served as Indian fighters in Texas, New Mexico, Kansas, Oklahoma, Nebraska, Utah, and Montana. Their chief opponents were the Apache Indians.

■ The 10th Cavalry was formed at Fort Leavenworth, Kansas, in 1866. They patrolled Kansas, Oklahoma, New Mexico, and Arizona where they fought against the Sioux, the Apache, and the Comanche. They were instrumental in the capture of the Apache chief Geronimo.

■ The 24th Infantry was formed in 1869 out of remnants of earlier infantry units.

■ The 25th Infantry was organized in the city of New Orleans in 1869.

■ Colonel John Pershing and future president Theodore Roosevelt led units from the 9th and 10th Cavalries in their famous charge up San Juan Hill in 1898 during the Spanish-American

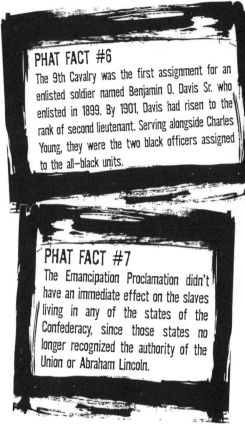

**PHAT FACT #6**

The 9th Cavalry was the first assignment for an enlisted soldier named Benjamin O. Davis Sr. who enlisted in 1899. By 1901, Davis had risen to the rank of second lieutenant. Serving alongside Charles Young, they were the two black officers assigned to the all-black units.

**PHAT FACT #7**

The Emancipation Proclamation didn't have an immediate effect on the slaves living in any of the states of the Confederacy, since those states no longer recognized the authority of the Union or Abraham Lincoln.

## Did you know...?

General George Armstrong Custer refused to be assigned to an all-black unit, but he did request that black trooper Isaiah Dorman be assigned to him as an interpreter of the Sioux language. Dorman died with Custer and the 7th Cavalry at the famous battle of Little Big Horn in 1876.

## Did you know...?

Colonel John Pershing—who rose to the rank of general—was willing to be the commanding officer of the all-black 10th Cavalry. That is how he earned the nickname "Black Jack" Pershing.

War. West Point trailblazer Charles Young also took part in that famous battle.

■ These all-black units made up 20 percent of the American military presence in the West and Southwest from 1870 to 1900.

▶▶**Fast Forward to 1940 and World War II:**

**BENJAMIN O. DAVIS SR.**

In 1940, Benjamin O. Davis Sr. became the first black brigadier general in U.S. military history. His son, Benjamin O. Davis Jr., achieved the even higher rank of major gen-

eral. He was the commanding officer of the famed Tuskegee Airmen of World War II—the first black pilots in the Army Air Corps, which would later become the U.S. Air Force.

**PHAT FACT #8**

Slaves living in the Confederate states only benefited from the Emancipation Proclamation if the Union army invaded their area and set them free.

**Did you know...?**

While slavery did not actually end with the issuing of the Emancipation Proclamation, the proclamation did mark a change in President Lincoln's position that he would try to save the Union without ending slavery.

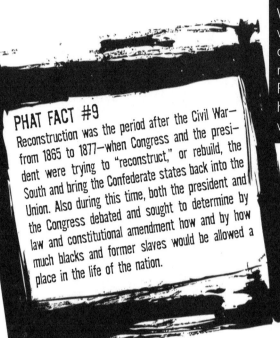

**PHAT FACT #9**

Reconstruction was the period after the Civil War—from 1865 to 1877—when Congress and the president were trying to "reconstruct," or rebuild, the South and bring the Confederate states back into the Union. Also during this time, both the president and the Congress debated and sought to determine by law and constitutional amendment how and by how much blacks and former slaves would be allowed a place in the life of the nation.

The Thirteenth Amendment to the U.S. Constitution states, "Neither slavery nor involuntary servitude... shall exist within the United States, or any place subject to their jurisdiction."

### The Emancipation Proclamation

**WHEN?** Issued on January 1, 1863.
**WHO?** By President Abraham Lincoln.
**WHAT?** Presidential action declaring freedom (emancipation) of slaves in specific states.
**WHERE?** Presidential action declaring slaves in states that had seceded from the Union were declared free as of January 1, 1863.
**EXCEPTIONS?** 1. Did not apply to the states of Missouri, Kentucky, Maryland, Delaware, and West Virginia—the "border states"—nor to Tennessee (which by that time was again under Union control) and parts of Louisiana and Virginia.
2. Did not apply to slaves living in Union states.
**RESULT?** The Emancipation Proclamation had the effect of causing tens of thousands of free blacks, runaway slaves, and slaves set free by the Union army to join the military in support of the Union.

## The 411 on the Freedmen's Bureau

■ Created in 1865
■ Intended to last only one year
■ Despite President Andrew Jackson's veto in 1866, Congress voted to keep the bureau in business until 1872
■ Formed Mission: to help former slaves in their transition to freedom and to help Southern whites loyal to the Union who had been left homeless by the Civil War
■ Distributed food, clothes, and other supplies
■ Built hospitals and schools throughout the former Confederacy
■ Looked over labor contracts between former slaves and their current employers
■ Instituted a judicial system used mainly to settle disagreements between former slaves and their employers

## Did you know...?

The Thirteenth Amendment to the U.S. Constitution, which ended legalized slavery in the United States, was ratified in the year 1865.

President Andrew Johnson vetoed the Civil Rights Act of 1866 because he believed that "Negroes are not yet ready for the privileges and equalities of citizens."

## Did you know...?

Because of the work of the Freedman's Bureau more than three thousand schools were built, more than nine thousand teachers were hired, and the first historically black colleges were started in the South.

## Did you know...?

The Fourteenth Amendment to the U.S. Constitution, ratified in 1868, secured the full citizenship rights of black people in the United States and also secured their right to seek justice through the court system.

## The Civil Rights Act of 1866

**WHAT?** The Civil Rights Act of 1866, passed by Congress, strengthened the Thirteenth Amendment by defining all persons born in the United States (except Native Americans) as national citizens and spelling out rights they were to enjoy equally without regard to race.
**WHAT WERE THESE RIGHTS?** These rights included the right to make contracts, the right to bring lawsuits, and the right to benefit from laws that protect individuals and their property.
**WHAT HAPPENED?** President Andrew Johnson vetoed the bill.
**THEN WHAT?** Congress passed the bill anyway.
**HOW?** By having enough votes to override—or set aside—the presidential veto.

The Fourteenth Amendment to the U.S. Constitution says, "...nor shall any State deprive any person of life, liberty, or property, without due process of law; nor deny to any person within its jurisdiction the equal protection of the law."

PHAT FACT #10
The Fifteenth Amendment did not grant the right to vote to women.

The Fifteenth Amendment to the U.S. Constitution says, "The right of citizens of the United States to vote shall not be denied or abridged by the United States or by any State on account of race, color, or previous condition of servitude."

### Did you know...?

The last of the Reconstruction amendments, the Fifteenth Amendment was ratified in 1870, granting the right to vote to all citizens.

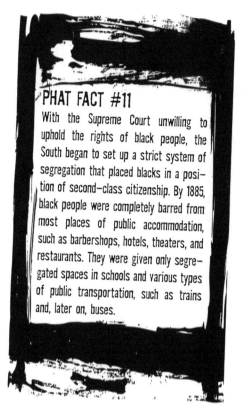

**PHAT FACT #11**

With the Supreme Court unwilling to uphold the rights of black people, the South began to set up a strict system of segregation that placed blacks in a position of second-class citizenship. By 1885, black people were completely barred from most places of public accommodation, such as barbershops, hotels, theaters, and restaurants. They were given only segregated spaces in schools and various types of public transportation, such as trains and, later on, buses.

▶▶**Fast Forward to 1920:**
**NINETEENTH AMENDMENT**
Women did not receive the right to vote for another fifty years, when the Nineteenth Amendment to the U.S. Constitution was ratified in 1920.

*More about the Civil Rights Act of 1875*

■ The United States Supreme Court—the highest ranking federal court in the country—declared the Civil Rights Act of 1875 unconstitutional.
■ The Supreme Court explained that the law was a violation of the Tenth Amendment of the U.S. Constitution and the right of states to enforce laws involving the citizens of those states.

## The 411 on the Civil Rights Act of 1875

■ Passed in an attempt to expand the rights and liberties of the former slaves who were still facing discrimination throughout the South
■ Made it illegal to discriminate in inns (today we call them hotels and motels), on modes of transportation, and in places of amusement that are open to the public
■ Made segregation illegal in places such as cemeteries, schools, and in jury selection at trials
■ Served as a promise of hope for African Americans because of black integration into every aspect of social, political, and economic life throughout the nation
■ Was unacceptable for many whites and was met with immediate, often violent, resistance, especially by those who had been part of the Confederate states or were former slave owners

■ This meant that it was not legal for the 1875 law to allow the federal government to protect the rights given to black people.

■ Instead, it was up to each state to enforce the laws that would guarantee rights to black people in each of those states.

## Plessy v. Ferguson
## Separate but Not_Equal

■ The United States Supreme Court's 1896 decision in *Plessy v. Ferguson* said that "separate but equal" accommodations between blacks and whites was allowed by the U.S. Constitution.

■ This ruling upheld the many forms of racial segregation that went into effect after the Civil Rights Act of 1875 was declared unconstitutional by the Supreme Court.

■ The case started in Louisiana where a fair-skinned black man named Homer Plessy was arrested for riding in the "white section" of a railroad car in violation of the Louisiana separate car law.

■ Plessy purposely sat in the "white section" as part of the plan by a group in the city of New Orleans known as the Citizens' Committee to Test the Constitutionality of the Separate Car Law.

■ Plessy made sure that the conductor on the train knew that he was of mixed racial heritage, which was enough to label him as black.

■ When arrested, Plessy argued that the segregation law in Louisiana was a violation of the protections guaranteed him by the Thirteenth and Fourteenth Amendments of the U.S. Constitution.

■ The U.S. Supreme Court did not accept Plessy's arguments. The

Supreme Court ruled that the Louisiana segregation law did not violate the Thirteenth Amendment, because the practice of slavery that was banned by that amendment was not being reintroduced.

■ The Supreme Court also ruled that the state of Louisiana was not breaking the law if the separate accommodations offered to black people were equal to the accommodations offered to whites.

## EARLY BLACK MIGRATION
### The Exodusters

■ Benjamin "Pop" Singleton and Henry Adams, both former slaves, formed a group known as the Exodusters in the 1870s.

■ The Exodusters took their name from the Bible and the people of Israel whose exodus from slavery in Egypt to freedom in the Promised Land reflected the hope of these former black slaves.

■ The Exodusters were a group of six thousand ex-slaves from the former slaveholding states of

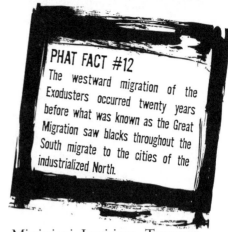

**PHAT FACT #12**

The westward migration of the Exodusters occurred twenty years before what was known as the Great Migration saw blacks throughout the South migrate to the cities of the industrialized North.

Mississippi, Louisiana, Tennessee, and Texas who migrated to the state of Kansas.

■ Both Singleton and Adams were convinced that the only hope available to black people living in the former Confederate states was to leave as quickly as possible to begin new lives in another part of the United States.

■ The Exodusters were fleeing the unrelenting violence of Southern whites who wanted to reassert their authority over them.

■ The Exodusters felt that the state of Kansas offered the best hope and the cheapest available land.

■ The group purchased plots of land on which they hoped to

When the Plessy v. Ferguson ruling was handed down in 1896, the only justice sitting on the U.S. Supreme Court who disagreed with the ruling was Justice John Marshall Harlan. He wrote, "Our Constitution is color-blind, and neither knows nor tolerates classes among citizens. In respect of civil rights, all citizens are equal before the law."

Frederick Douglass and other black leaders at the time opposed the Exoduster migration. They insisted that it was the duty of the federal government to protect black citizens where they lived, including in the states of the former confederacy. Douglass also feared that by leaving the place where they had lived for so many generations, blacks in the West might become "nomads," forever wandering through strange territory and never really settling down.

build homes and establish farms, businesses, and eventually all-black communities.

PHAT FACT #13
Du Bois died in Accra, Ghana, on August 27, 1963, the same day as the March on Washington where Martin Luther King Jr. delivered his "I have a dream" speech.

■ Traveling by wagon, they made their way, first, to St. Louis, Missouri, where they restocked their wagons. Then they traveled on to their homesteads in Kansas.

■ The Exoduster movement became so popular that it was known as "Kansas fever."

▶▶Fast Forward to 1954:
## BROWN V. BOARD OF EDUCATION

The practice of "separate but equal" would be the law of the land until it was overturned by the 1954 U.S. Supreme Court decision in Brown v. Board of Education, which outlawed segregation in public education.

### THE GREAT DEBATE

**W. E. B. Du Bois and Booker T. Washington** held very different ideas on how best to lift up and improve the lives of blacks in the years after slavery. Washington advocated industrial education and training that would equip black people to become self-sufficient through manual and domestic labor. In contrast, Du Bois was the primary creator of a philosophy called "the talented tenth." That phrase referred to a special group of black people who would be trained in the liberal arts and prepared for professions such as medicine, education, and law. Their success and accomplishments would then inspire other blacks to higher levels of achievement.

Du Bois and Washington also differed on the issue of political

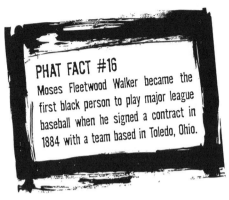

**PHAT FACT #16**
Moses Fleetwood Walker became the first black person to play major league baseball when he signed a contract in 1884 with a team based in Toledo, Ohio.

activity and the right to vote. Du Bois outspokenly advocated that black people should agitate until the right to vote was restored. He felt that the right to vote was guaranteed by the Fifteenth Amendment even though it was not enforced after the Civil Rights Act of 1875 was ruled unconstitutional. Washington, on the other hand, in his famous 1895 speech at the Atlanta Exposition, tried to strike a bargain with whites in the South, saying that if they would be willing to assist black people in gaining economic advancement, blacks should respond by abandoning any further activity to regain the right to vote.

## The 411 on W. E. B. Du Bois

■ Born in Great Barrington, Massachusetts, on February 23, 1868
■ Earned a second Bachelor of Arts after earning his first degree from Fisk University in Nashville, Tennessee, in 1888
■ In 1895, became the first black person to earn a PhD from Harvard University
■ Also studied history and economics at the University of Berlin from 1892 to 1894
■ Taught at Fisk University, Wilberforce University, and the University of Pennsylvania from 1894 to 1897, and at Atlanta University from 1897 to 1910
■ Retired from teaching and from 1910 to 1934 served as editor of *Crisis*, the monthly journal of the NAACP
■ Joined the Communist Party in 1961
■ Also in 1961, emigrated to and became an official citizen of Ghana in West Africa

W. E. B. Du Bois is most often remembered for comments he made in his classic essay collection THE SOULS OF BLACK FOLK:

"One ever feels (one's) two-ness,—an American, a Negro; two souls, two thoughts, two unreconciled strivings; two warring ideals in one dark body."

"The black preacher is the most unique personality developed by the Negro on American soil....He early appeared on the plantation and found his function as the healer of the sick, the interpreter of the Unknown, the comforter of the sorrowing, the supernatural avenger of wrong, and the one who rudely but picturesquely expressed the longing, disappointment, and resentment of a stolen and oppressed people."

"The problem of the twentieth century is the problem of the color-line, the relation of the darker to the lighter races of men in Asia and Africa, in America and the islands of the sea."

**More about W. E. B. Du Bois**
Du Bois was the author of several books, including: *The Philadelphia Negro, The Suppression of the Slave Trade, The Souls of Black Folk,* as well as *Black Reconstruction.*

**More about Booker T. Washington**
Washington was the author of several books, including: *The Negro in Business, The Story of the Negro, The Story of My Life and Work,* and *Up from Slavery* (autobiography).

## The 411 on Booker T. Washington

■ Born in 1856, the last of the great African American leaders to have been born in slavery

■ After Civil War, in 1865, was taken by his mother, along with his siblings, to Malden, West Virginia, where his mother's husband was living

■ Worked grueling hours in a salt mine and then found work as a houseboy

■ At age sixteen, walked across Virginia to attend Hampton Normal and Agricultural Institute

■ At Hampton met the person who would have the greatest influence on his life: General Samuel Chapman Armstrong, one of the Hampton Institute founders

■ After finishing studies at Hampton Institute, returned to Malden, Virginia, to teach for one year

■ Then attended Wayland Seminary in Washington, D.C., but left after one year, unhappy with the lack of the kind of physical work required of students at Hampton Institute

■ Returned to Hampton Institute and worked as a housefather for a dormitory

■ In 1881—on the recommendation of General Armstrong—left for Tuskegee, Alabama, to start school based on Hampton Institute model

■ Founded Tuskegee Institute in 1881 to equip students for careers in mechanical, industrial, and agricultural sciences

■ By 1888, school owned five hundred acres of land and enrolled five hundred students

■ At Washington's death in 1915, school had an endowment of $2 million, a staff of two hundred, and two thousand students

■ First black person to create a successful, ongoing institution outside of the church—Tuskegee Institute

▶▶Fast Forward to 1947:
**JACKIE ROBINSON**

When Jackie Robinson played the 1947 season with the Brooklyn Dodgers, he became the first black person to play in the major leagues since Moses Fleetwood Walker in 1884.

▶▶Fast Forward to 1929:
**ABYSSINIAN BAPTIST CHURCH**

During the Great Depression (1929–1939), the Abyssinian Baptist Church operated a soup kitchen and offered other social services. At Adam Clayton Powell Sr.'s retirement in 1937, he had

**Did you know...?**

When James Augustine Healy was named bishop of the diocese of Portland, Maine, by Pope Pious IX, he was the first black person ever appointed as a bishop in the history of the Roman Catholic Church in the United States. As bishop, he built sixty-five mission stations, eighteen Catholic schools, and sixty-five new church buildings. His diocese was also expanded to include all of New Hampshire and parts of Massachusetts.

## The 411 on Hiram Revels

- Born free in Fayetteville, North Carolina, in 1822
- Entered ministry of African Methodist Episcopal Church at age twenty-five
- Served as recruiter for first all-black regiments from Missouri and Maryland for Union army during Civil War
- Appointed by President Lincoln to be a military chaplain and served some all-black regiments
- After war, settled in Mississippi and was appointed to state legislature in 1867; appointed to U.S. Senate in 1870
- Became first black person to serve in U.S. Senate when sworn in on February 25, 1870, to represent the state of Mississippi
- After fourteen months' service in Senate, became president of all-black Alcorn A&M University in Mississippi, oldest U.S. land grant college for blacks
- Died in 1901

built that church into the largest Protestant congregation in the world, with more than fourteen thousand members. He had built a megachurch seventy years before the term became popular!

## NEW RELIGIOUS ORGANIZATIONS IN THE NINETEENTH CENTURY

**Colored Methodist Episcopal** (CME) Church was organized in Jackson, Tennessee, in 1870. (The name was changed to the Christian Methodist Episcopal in 1957). Most of the black Methodists who organized the CME Church had been members of the Methodist Episcopal Church of the South (which split from the Methodist Episcopal Church in 1844 over the question of slavery). The founders of the

## The 411 on Adam Clayton Powell Sr.

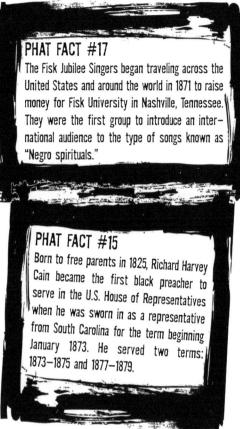

- In 1865, born in Franklin County, Virginia
- Son of an African-Cherokee woman and a German-born slave owner
- In 1892, graduated from Wayland Seminary in Washington, D.C.
- Served as pastor of several churches before becoming pastor of the Abyssinian Baptist Church in New York City in 1908

## The 411 on Charles Thomas (C.T.) Walker

- Born into slavery in 1858, in Hephzibah, Georgia
- Acknowledged a call to ministry and enrolled in the Augusta Institute (which later relocated to Atlanta and became Morehouse College)
- Ordained in 1877 and served several churches before beginning ministry at Tabernacle Baptist Church, Augusta, Georgia
- Quickly became one of the most famous and highly sought-after African American preachers in the United States
- In 1895, appointed by President William McKinley to be army chaplain to African American soldiers serving in Cuba during Spanish-American War
- Also became a force within the newly formed National Baptist Convention USA.
- Referred to as "the black Spurgeon," comparing the power and popularity of his preaching with that of the British preacher Charles Haddon Spurgeon, who was believed by many to be the nineteenth-century's greatest preacher

CME Church also included many persons who had been enslaved prior to the end of the Civil War. Once they gained freedom, they wanted to remain Methodist, but as an independent group.

**Church of God in Christ** (COGIC) was founded in 1897 as a Holiness movement by Charles Harrison Mason and Charles Price Jones, Baptist pastors who believed that a person's initial conversion to Christ must be followed by a second step called "sanctification" or "being filled with the Holy Spirit." The COGIC was initially a movement within the Baptist faith, but Mason and Price were expelled from the National Baptist convention in 1899 over their insistence on the doctrine of sanctification as a necessary step for salvation.

However in 1907, Mason traveled to Los Angeles to attend the Azusa Street revival that was being led by another black

## Did you know...?

The National Baptist Convention of the United States of America was formed in 1895 in Atlanta, Georgia, representing the merger of three black Baptist organizations already in existence—the National Baptist Educational Convention, the Baptist Foreign Mission Board, and the American National Baptist Convention. A national black Baptist organization was formed because the white dominated Southern Baptist Convention made it clear that it was not interested in or willing to allow any meaningful opportunities for blacks within its structure.

preacher. He had a Pentecostal experience in which he began to speak in tongues. That experience reshaped his core beliefs to include speaking in tongues as a sign of the baptism in the Holy Spirit. Jones, who did not attend the revival, did not agree with Mason on the need to speak in tongues, and the two men split over this issue. Mason continued to use the name Church of God in Christ, and Jones started the Church of Christ (Holiness), USA.

## The 411 on Dr. Daniel Hale Williams

- Born in Pennsylvania in 1856
- Graduated from the Chicago Medical College in 1883
- In 1891, established the Provident Hospital in Chicago, a place where black doctors could admit their patients and where their patients would be treated without facing racial discrimination
- In 1893, became the first person to successfully operate on a human heart
- In 1893, called to treat a patient who had been stabbed in an artery a fraction of an inch from the heart. Opened the man's chest cavity, sewed the wound, and saved his life instead of giving the patient pain medication so that he could die peacefully
- Went on to transform the Howard University Hospital and either created or helped to create more than forty hospitals that served black communities across the country

# Section 4
## Changing Times (1900–1950)

### Revolution, Renaissance, and Racism

The period from 1900 to 1950 was a time of fast-paced change in the United States that affected the lives of most African Americans. The rise of the industrial revolution created new economic opportunities for Americans, especially African Americans; blacks left the South in great numbers for new lives in the urban centers of the North.

The Harlem Renaissance during the 1920s marked a time of artistic and intellectual passion for black Americans not just in Harlem but across the United States. The number of blacks expressing themselves as artists, authors, photographers, and musicians reached numbers that had never been seen in this country up to that time. In addition, there was a greater appreciation for that work within the general population.

While blacks also saw a rise in opportunities available to them, the ugly realities of racism continued to seek to hold back those advancements. While the American legal system was increasingly turned to by blacks and sympathetic whites as a means of righting the wrongs of discrimination, lynchings—hangings that were carried out outside of the legal system, usually by mobs of angry white people—were a frequent and brutal reality for African Americans, mainly in the South.

Even though the U.S. Constitution had been amended so that blacks (males) were given the right to vote, in the South, blacks who attempted to exercise that right on voting day were often required to pass tests that no white citizens were asked to take. When that failed, Southern whites often resorted to violence.

## RELIGION AND BLACK AMERICA

**Howard Thurman** was born in 1900 in Daytona Beach, Florida, graduated from Morehouse College in 1923 and Rochester (New York) Theological Seminary in 1926. He taught at Morehouse College from 1930 to 1932 and then became dean of the chapel at Howard University. After traveling to India in 1935 to meet the internationally respected pacifist and nonviolent protester Mahatma Gandhi, Thurman returned to the United States committed to the principles of nonviolence and nonviolent protest. In 1944, he became the founding pastor of the Church for the Fellowship of All Peoples in San Francisco, an interracial congregation.

▶▶**Fast Forward to 1953:**
**HOWARD THURMAN**
**In 1953 Howard Thurman became the first black man in American history to be appointed to an administrative position in a major research university when he was appointed dean of the chapel at Boston University.**

**That same year, *Life* magazine named Thurman one of the twelve greatest preachers of the twentieth century. In 1954, *Ebony* magazine listed him as one of the ten most outstanding black preachers in America.**

**Thurman retired from Boston University in 1965.**

*More about Howard Thurman*
In 1945 he wrote *Deep River*, the first of twenty books. He also wrote *The Negro Speaks of Life and Death*, based on his 1947 Ingersoll Lectures at Harvard Divinity School. His autobiography is titled *With Head and Heart.*

**Clarence LaVaughn (C. L.) Franklin** was born in 1915 in Sunflower County, Mississippi. He began as a sharecropper and migrant worker, but by the end of his life he was one of the most widely heard and imitated black preachers in the country. His church began a radio broadcast in 1951, and he was one of the first black preachers to use radio to reach a wider

audience. Franklin expanded his reach even further when he also had his sermons recorded and distributed by the Chess Recording Company of Chicago. His recordings sold more than one million copies. He preached across the country for fifteen years before serving the rest of his ministry years at New Bethel Baptist Church in Detroit.

**Gardner C. Taylor** was born in Baton Rouge, Louisiana, in 1918. After his graduation from Leland College in Baker, Louisiana, he was accepted into the University of Michigan School of Law. However, in 1937, after a terrible

car accident, he changed his plans and decided on a career in the ministry. He graduated from Oberlin School of Theology in Ohio in 1940. After serving at two other churches, in 1948, he was called to be the pastor of Concord Baptist Church in Brooklyn, New York, where he remained until his retirement in 1990. In 1961, Gardner Taylor joined with Martin Luther King Jr. and other socially progressive pastors to found the Progressive National Baptist Convention. At the height of his career in the ministry, he was called the "dean" of black preachers by *Time*

executive order: an order from the president of the United States having the power and effect of a law

Great Depression: the period from the end of 1929 and continuing through approximately 1941 when American prosperity came to a halt—businesses and banks closed, unemployment rose dramatically, and many families lost their homes and savings

interracial: having or involving more than one race

pacifist: someone who believes that disagreements between nations should never be solved by going to war

renaissance: a time of revived or renewed artistic and intellectual achievement

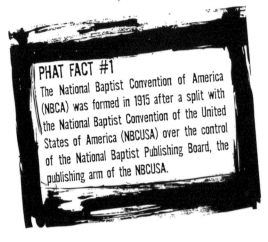

**PHAT FACT #1**
The National Baptist Convention of America (NBCA) was formed in 1915 after a split with the National Baptist Convention of the United States of America (NBCUSA) over the control of the National Baptist Publishing Board, the publishing arm of the NBCUSA.

1960s. Taylor's sermons were broadcast along with those of such prominent preachers as Harry Emerson Fosdick, Ralph Sockman, and Paul Scherer.

▶▶**Fast Forward to 2000: GARDNER TAYLOR**
**President Bill Clinton awarded Gardner Taylor the Presidential Medal of Freedom, the highest nonmilitary honor the nation can bestow upon one of its citizens.**

magazine and twice was listed in *Ebony* magazine as the top black preacher in America.

**More about Gardner C. Taylor**

■ Taylor has written several books, including *How Shall They Preach*, *The Scarlet Thread*, and *We Have This Ministry* (coauthored with Samuel Dewitt Proctor).

■ Taylor preached over the NBC television network's National Radio Pulpit in the 1950s and

Charles Emanuel ("Daddy") Grace was born in 1895 in Cape Verde, West Africa. He worked a variety of odd jobs until he made the claim in 1920 that—having just returned from the Holy Land (Israel and the Palestinian territories)—he had healed people of a wide variety of diseases. That was the beginning of his ministry.

## The Great Migration

**WHAT?** The movement of more than four million African Americans from the rural areas of the South to the industrial centers of the North—New York, Chicago, Detroit, Cleveland, and Pittsburgh.
**WHEN?** Between 1895 and 1945.
**WHY?** To escape the often violent racial oppression in the South; also because the sharecropping system of the South resembled a form of slavery, with black farm workers finding it almost impossible to get ahead financially and economically. The steel mills, meatpacking plants, automobile factories, and other manufacturing plants proved to be a strong attraction for African Americans looking for a better life.

## The 411 on Elijah Muhammad

- Born in 1897 in Sandersville, Georgia
- Named Elijah Poole at birth
- Migrated to Detroit, Michigan, in 1923, where he worked in the auto industry
- Met Wallace D. Fard in 1930
- Joined the recently organized Nation of Islam and quickly rose to second in command
- Renamed Elijah Muhammad by Fard
- After Fard's disappearance in 1934, moved to Chicago and soon took control of the movement
- Gave himself the title of "Messenger of Allah"
- Began to establish other temples across the country
- Concentrated on northern cities among blacks who were disenchanted with the American dream or who had been incarcerated

Within two years he had established a large following along the East Coast. His services followed the Pentecostal worship traditions except for one major exception:

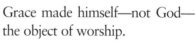

### Did you know…?

Wentworth Arthur Matthew, was born in 1892 in Nigeria and later immigrated to the United States. He became the leader of a black Jewish community known as both The Commandment Keepers and the Black Jews of Harlem. At its peak, membership was 3,000 in New York City. There are several congregations of black Jews across the U.S. today.

Grace made himself—not God— the object of worship.

**Adam Clayton Powell Jr.** was born in New Haven, Connecticut, in 1908. Powell graduated from Colgate University in Hamilton, New York, in 1930. He attended Union Theological Seminary in New York City before transferring to Columbia University where he earned a Master of Arts in religion in 1931. He served as assistant pastor of his father's church, Absysinian Baptist Church in New York City, from 1931 to 1937. He became senior pastor of the church in 1937. In 1941, Powell began his political career by being the first black person ever elected to the city council of New York City. In 1945 he was elected to the first of eleven terms as a member of the U.S. House of Representatives.

More about Adam Clayton Powell Jr.

In 1945, when Powell was elected to his first term in the U.S. House of Representatives, he quickly developed the "Powell Amendment," which he added to any bills proposing federal funding for the construction of schools. The amendment called for the withholding of any

funding from a local or state agency that practiced discrimination against blacks when hiring. The amendment was used to withhold federal funds from schools that continued to practice segregation after the landmark school segregation ruling in *Brown v. Board of Education* in 1954.

▶▶**Fast Forward to 1961: ADAM CLAYTON POWELL JR. Adam Clayton Powell Jr. reached the height of his political power in 1961 when he became chair of the Education and Labor Committee of the House of Representatives.**

**In 1970 Powell lost his seat in the House of Representatives when he was defeated in his bid for a twelfth term in Congress by Charles Rangel.**

### The Nation of Islam

The roots of the Nation of Islam can be traced to a black American who was named Timothy Drew at his birth in North Carolina in 1886 but who later became known as Noble Drew Ali. He began preaching his message that black Americans should convert from Christianity to Islam when he organized the first Moorish Science Temple in Newark, New Jersey, in 1913. Within a few years he had established temples in Pittsburgh, Philadelphia, Detroit, and Chicago.

While it is believed that Ali developed a following of around twenty thousand persons, he is best known for being the first black American leader to make the claim that Christianity is the religion for white people (Europeans) and that all black people should convert to Islam.

### More about the Nation of Islam

■ Wallace D. Fard was born in 1877. While he claimed to be from the holy city of Mecca in Saudi Arabia, his actual birthplace is thought to have been Jamaica, New Zealand, or Portland, Oregon. It is widely believed that Fard was a follower of Noble Drew Ali. In 1930, Fard began a movement known as The Lost-Found Nation of Islam in Detroit, Michigan.

■ Among the people who responded to Fard's message was Elijah Poole, whose name was changed by Fard to Elijah Muhammad. Together they set out to build a movement that would become the Nation of Islam.

## BREAKING THE COLOR LINE IN SPORTS

**John Arthur (Jack) Johnson** defeated Tommy Burns in a boxing match in Sydney, Australia, in 1908, becoming the first black man ever to hold the title of heavyweight champion of the world. Born in Galveston, Texas, in 1878, Jack

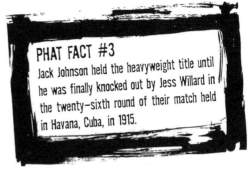

PHAT FACT #3
Jack Johnson held the heavyweight title until he was finally knocked out by Jess Willard in the twenty-sixth round of their match held in Havana, Cuba, in 1915.

Johnson began fighting professionally in 1897. He was constantly denied an opportunity to fight for the heavyweight championship until his match against Burns.

▶▶**Fast Forward to 1968:**
**JACK JOHNSON**
**The Broadway show (1968) and subsequent movie (1970)** *The Great White Hope*, **both starring award-winning actor James Earl Jones, were based on the life of Jack Johnson.**

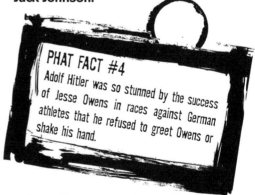

PHAT FACT #4
Adolf Hitler was so stunned by the success of Jesse Owens in races against German athletes that he refused to greet Owens or shake his hand.

**Jesse Owens** was born James Cleveland Owens in Oakville, Alabama, in 1913. He attended Ohio State University in 1933 but did not receive an athletic scholarship. At a Big Ten track meet in Ann

**PHAT FACT #5**
The Tuskegee Airmen were under the command of Colonel Benjamin O. Davis Jr., a West Point graduate (class of 1932) who went on to become the first black person to attain the rank of a three-star major general in the U.S. Army.

Arbor, Michigan, in 1935, Owens set three world records and tied a fourth. In 1936, Owens qualified for four Olympic events and went on to win four gold medals in the 1936 Olympic Games held in Berlin, Germany. He won the 100- and 200-meter events and the broad jump (now called the long jump) and shared in the 400-meter relay.

▶▶**Fast Forward to 1976:**
**JESSE OWENS**

**Jesse Owens was awarded the Presidential Medal of Freedom by President Gerald Ford in 1976.**

**Marion Motley, Bill Willis, Kenny Washington, and Woody Strode** became the first black players in modern professional football in 1946. Motley and Willis played for the Cleveland Browns in the newly formed All-America football conference. Washington and Strode signed with the Los Angeles Rams in the National Football League. Of these four athletes, Motley and Willis achieved Hall of Fame

careers. Washington played three seasons in the NFL, and Strode played one NFL season.

*More about Marion Motley*
■ Averaged 5.7 yards per carry as a runner
■ Named All-Pro fullback when the All-American Football Conference merged with the National Football League in 1950–51
■ Played for the NFL until 1953
■ Inducted into the Pro Football Hall of Fame in 1968

**Jackie Robinson** was born Jack Roosevelt Robinson in 1919 near Cairo, Georgia, he became the first black person signed in the twentieth century to play professional baseball in the major leagues when he joined the Brooklyn Dodgers. Robinson attended Pasadena Junior College from 1937 to 1939, then transferred to the University of California in Los Angeles on an athletic scholarship to play baseball and football. He left college before graduating. After a stint in the army, Robinson signed a contract to play baseball with the Kansas City Monarchs of the Negro Baseball League. Later in 1945, Robinson signed a contract to play for the Montreal Royals, a minor league team for the Brooklyn Dodgers. In 1947,

Robinson was called up to the Dodgers and broke the color barrier in major league baseball.

*More about Jackie Robinson...*

■ Named Major League Baseball's Rookie of the Year in 1947

■ Named Most Valuable Player in the National League in 1949

■ Inducted into the Baseball Hall of Fame in 1962

## CHANGES IN THE MILITARY

The Tuskegee Airmen were formed as an all-black squadron of fighter pilots in 1941 and were the first black pilots in the history of the U.S. Armed Forces. Their name came from their training camp which was on the campus of Tuskegee Institute.

The Tuskegee Airmen consisted of 992 pilots who were assigned to the 99th, 100th, 301st, and 302nd combat units. Of this group, 450 were sent overseas for combat missions. The Airmen were not only pilots, however. The group included mechanics, ground crew, gunners, armorers, and flight engineers. Together they maintained and helped to operate the airplanes.

In 1944, the four units of the Tuskegee Airmen were merged into the 332nd Fighter Group and given the assignment of escorting bombing planes during their bombing runs over German-occupied areas of Italy, France, and even Berlin, Germany. As

*Did you know...?*

Sixty-six Tuskegee Airmen were killed in action. The unit won more than 100 Distinguished Flying Crosses and three Distinguished Unit Citations.

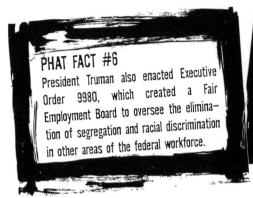

**PHAT FACT #6**
President Truman also enacted Executive Order 9980, which created a Fair Employment Board to oversee the elimination of segregation and racial discrimination in other areas of the federal workforce.

**PHAT FACT #7**
Benjamin E. Mays was the author of two thousand articles and nine books, including *The Negro's Church* (coauthored with Joseph W. Nicholson), *Concerned about Man*, and *Born to Rebel* (autobiography).

escorts, they protected the bombing planes from enemy aircraft in the air as well as planes still on the ground—and even a naval ship—that would try to keep the American bombers from successfully completing their missions.

The 332nd Fighter Group of the Tuskegee Airmen was involved in 1,578 combat missions during which they shot down 111 enemy aircraft, sank a German naval ship, and destroyed more than 150 other German planes that were still on the ground. The Tuskegee Airmen's greatest accomplishment is that they never lost to enemy aircraft a single bomber plane that was assigned to them.

**Executive Order 9981** issued in 1948 by United States president Harry S. Truman, which called for the end of racial segregation in all branches of the U.S. military. Tru-

## The 411 on Benjamin E. Mays

■ Born in 1894 near Epworth, South Carolina
■ Phi Beta Kappa (honor) graduate of Bates College in Lewiston, Maine
■ Earned MA (1925) and PhD (1935) from University of Chicago
■ Before becoming Morehouse president, taught on faulty at Morehouse (1921–1924) and South Carolina State College
■ Spent six years as dean of the School of Religion at Howard University in Washington, D.C.
■ Received a lifetime total of fifty-six honorary doctoral degrees

The inscription on the tombstone of Benjamin E. Mays reads: "It must be borne in mind that the tragedy in life doesn't lie in not reaching your goal. The tragedy lies in having no goal to reach. It isn't a calamity to die with dreams unfulfilled, but it is a calamity not to dream. It is not a disaster to be unable to capture your ideal, but it is a disaster to have no ideal to capture. It is not a disgrace not to reach the stars, but it is a disgrace to have no stars to reach for. Not failure, but low aim is the sin."

man also created the President's Committee on Equality of Treatment and Opportunity in the Armed Services, a group whose job was to see that Truman's order to abolish segregation was carried out.

## TEACHERS AND SCHOLARS

**Benjamin E. Mays** served as president of Morehouse College in Atlanta, Georgia, from 1941 to 1967. From that position, he molded and mentored an entire generation of men who went on to become leaders in every area of American life. His most notable student was the Rev. Dr. Martin Luther King Jr. who graduated from Morehouse College in 1948.

▶▶**Fast Forward to 1970:**
**BENJAMIN E. MAYS**
In 1970, Benjamin E. Mays became the first black president of the Atlanta Board of Education where he served for twelve years.

**Mary McLeod Bethune** was born Mary McLeod in 1875 in Mayesville, South Carolina. In 1904, with $1.50 in her pocket and fruit crates to use as desks, she

### Did you know...?

Mary McLeod Bethune went to Moody College in Chicago in 1890, intending to become a missionary to Africa. The Board of Missions denied her application because they thought a black American missionary might create unrest among the African people she came in contact with.

PHAT FACT #8
In 1935, Mary McLeod Bethune was awarded the NAACP Spingarn Medal for her work as an educator.

▶▶Fast Forward to 1973:
**MARY McLEOD BETHUNE**
In 1973, a statue in Mary McLeod Bethune's honor was erected in Washington, D.C.'s Lincoln Park.

established the Normal and Industrial School for Young Negro Women in Daytona Beach, Florida. Within three years, the enrollment increased to 250 students. In 1923 the school merged with Cookman Institute, a school for boys, and became Bethune-Cookman College.

Mordecai Wyatt Johnson became the first black president of Howard University in Washington, D.C., in 1926. He was born in 1890 in Paris, Tennessee. Johnson graduated from Morehouse College in 1911 and began his career teaching economics and history at Morehouse College. He also earned a Bachelor of Arts from the

## The 411 on Mary McLeod Bethune

■ Enrolled at Scotia College in North Carolina in 1888
■ Enrolled in Moody Bible Institute in Chicago in 1890
■ Married Albertus Bethune in 1898
■ Relocated to Florida where she would soon open her girls' school
■ President of the National Association of Colored Women's Clubs (1924–1928)
■ Founder and president of the National Council of Negro Women (1935–1949)
■ Member of the "Black Cabinet," a group of influential black Americans who advised President Franklin Roosevelt on race relations
■ Director of Negro Affairs for the National Youth Administration (1936–1943), the first black woman to serve as the head of a federal agency

# The 411 on Mordecai Wyatt Johnson

- Following Mordecai Wyatt Johnson's historic appointment as the first black president of Howard University, for the next thirty-four years he redefined the role of a black college president and redefined the mission of Howard University. During his term as president, he accomplished the following:
- Increased the federal allocation to Howard University from $218,000 to $6 million per year
- Tripled the size of the faculty and doubled their salaries
- Attracted top scholars to head the various university departments, including Benjamin E. Mays as dean of the School of Religion, Carter G. Woodson as dean of the School of Liberal Arts, E. Franklin Frazier as chair of the Department of Sociology, and Charles Hamilton Houston as dean of the law school.
- Led Howard University Medical School in training half of all black doctors and dentists who graduated each year

PHAT FACT #9
Mordecai Wyatt Johnson was awarded the NAACP's prestigious Spingarn Medal in 1929.

University of Chicago in 1913, a Bachelor of Divinity from Rochester Theological Seminary in New York in 1916, and a Master of Sacred Theology from Harvard Divinity School in 1922.

**Carter G. Woodson** was born in 1875 in New Canton, Virginia. He earned a Bachelor of Arts from Berea College in Kentucky and a Master of Arts from the University of Chicago. In 1926, he became

*In his inaugural address as president of Howard University, Mordecai Wyatt Johnson said, "There is no organization and no combination of organizations now at work in the black community which can, at this state in the history of the Negro race, begin to compare with the fundamental importance of the Negro church."*

## The 411 on Carter G. Woodson

- Created the Association for the Study of Negro Life and History in 1916
- Organized Associated Publishers in 1921 so that materials by and about black people could be published
- Landmark book, *History of the Negro Church*, first book to be published by Associated Publishers
- Other books include *The Education of the Negro Prior to 1861* (1915), *A Century of Negro Migration* (1918), *The Negro in Our History* (1922), *The Rural Negro* (1930), and *The Miseducation of the Negro* (1933)

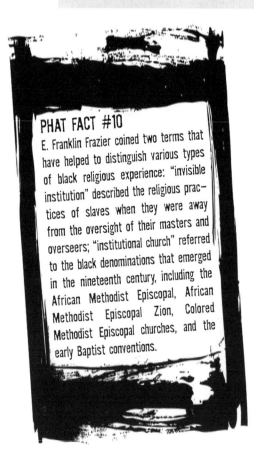

**PHAT FACT #10**

E. Franklin Frazier coined two terms that have helped to distinguish various types of black religious experience: "invisible institution" described the religious practices of slaves when they were away from the oversight of their masters and overseers; "institutional church" referred to the black denominations that emerged in the nineteenth century, including the African Methodist Episcopal, African Methodist Episcopal Zion, Colored Methodist Episcopal churches, and the early Baptist conventions.

the second African American to receive a Doctor of Philosophy from Harvard University. He also studied at the Sorbonne in Paris, France. In 1926, Woodson established Negro History Week, an observance that later (in 1976) was expanded to cover the month of February. That month was chosen because both Abraham Lincoln and Frederick Douglass were born in February.

**E. Franklin Frazier** was born in 1894 in Baltimore, Maryland. He earned a Bachelor of Arts from Howard University in 1916. He earned a Doctor of Philosophy from the University of Chicago and then spent twenty-five years as chair of the Sociology Department at Howard University.

## The 411 on E. Franklin Frazier

■ Awarded Guggenheim Fellowships in 1940 and 1941, which he used to study African life in Brazil and the West Indies
■ In 1948, chosen by peers to be president of the American Sociological Society
■ Author of many significant books, including *The Negro Family in the United States* (1939), *The Black Bourgeoisie* (1957), and *The Negro Church in America* (1961)

Frazier was at the center of an important discussion about whether any aspects of native African religious life and practice were able to survive the so-called Middle Passage (the route of the Atlantic slave trade which transported blacks from Africa to the New World) and the experience of centuries of slavery. Frazier argued that little, if anything, of Africa was able to survive that experience. Other scholars, including Melville Herkovits and W. E. B. Du Bois held to a different point of view, believing that African practices could be found in the Americas in those places where a substantial black majority existed.

*More about E. Franklin Frazier*
Frazier also argued that a loss of cultural memory occurred when black people migrated from the South in massive numbers to various urban centers in the North, just as he said occurred in the forced migration from their homeland in Africa to the Americas.

**Charles Drew** was born in 1904 in Washington, D.C. He graduated from Amherst College in Massachusetts, and then worked for a short time as a biology teacher and athletic director at Morgan State University in Baltimore,

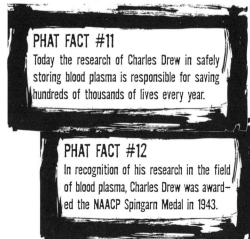

**PHAT FACT #11**
Today the research of Charles Drew in safely storing blood plasma is responsible for saving hundreds of thousands of lives every year.

**PHAT FACT #12**
In recognition of his research in the field of blood plasma, Charles Drew was awarded the NAACP Spingarn Medal in 1943.

# The 411 on Charles Drew

- After completing medical degree in 1933, returned to Washington, D.C., to teach pathology at Howard University Medical School
- Pursued a doctor of science degree at Columbia University in New York City
- Wrote dissertation at Columbia on storage of blood plasma
- Expertise in blood plasma led to appointment as director of American Red Cross Blood Bank in New York City
- Dissertation on storage of blood plasma caught British government's attention, and they sought his help in this area
- In 1940, supervised shipment of ten thousand pints of blood plasma to England during battle of Britain against the Nazis.
- Shortly after, moved to England to become medical director of Blood for Britain program; responsible for collection, storing, and distribution of blood plasma there during World War II

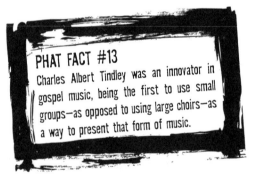

**PHAT FACT #13**
Charles Albert Tindley was an innovator in gospel music, being the first to use small groups—as opposed to using large choirs—as a way to present that form of music.

## THE ARTISTIC SCENE

**Charles Albert Tindley** was born into a slave family in Berlin, Maryland, sometime between 1851 and 1856. After emancipation, he moved to Philadelphia where he worked as a church caretaker. With no formal education, he began reading books in the church library and soon began to prepare himself for a career in the ministry. In 1900, Charles Albert Tindley became pastor of the same church where he had served as caretaker. The very next year, in 1901, he released his first of many popular hymns, "I'll Overcome Someday." His hymns

Maryland. He later enrolled in medical school at McGill University in Montreal, Canada. It was there that he began his research on the collection and storage of blood plasma, the product that makes blood transfusions possible.

have been translated into many foreign languages and appear in hymnals of nearly every denomination in the United States.

**More about Charles Albert Tindley**

In all, Tindley wrote forty-five hymns, including the old standards:

- "We'll Understand It Better By and By"
- "Nothing between My Soul and My Savior
- "The Storm Is Passing Over"
- "Beams of Heaven"
- "Take Your Burdens to the Lord and Leave Them There"
- "Stand By Me"

**Did you know...?**

Because of the enthusiastic receptions Paul Robeson received during his concert performances and visits to Russia, he spoke warmly about Russia and the Communist Party, which was enough to brand him a "Communist sympathizer" during his testimony before the House of Representatives' Un-American Activities Committee in 1947. Robeson's passport was taken away from 1947 to 1958, thereby ending his career.

**Paul Robeson** was born in Princeton, New Jersey, in 1898. A scholar as well as an athlete, Robeson graduated Phi Beta Kappa (with honors) as valedictorian (first in his class) from Rutgers University (New Jersey) in 1919. He enrolled in Columbia University Law School and finished in two years while also playing professional football to raise money for his tuition. He also raised money by singing in the chorus of a black-cast theater production in New York City.

Despite his excellent grades and multiple talents, none of the white law firms in New York City would hire him as a lawyer. Finally, Robeson decided to abandon his plans to be a lawyer and focus on a career as an actor and singer. He appeared on concert stages throughout Europe, becoming one of the highest paid performers in the world during the 1930s.

**More about Paul Robeson**

- Robeson appeared in major stage productions, such as Emperor Jones and Othello.
- He was most famous for his stage role in Showboat, in which he sang "Old Man River."
- He repeated those popular roles in Hollywood movies.

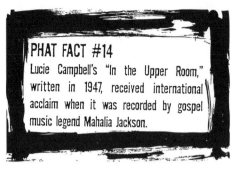
**Lucie Campbell** was the first woman to make an impact on gospel music in the black church. She was born in 1885 in Duck Hill, Mississippi, to parents who had formerly been slaves. She finished high school in Memphis, Tennessee, in 1899 at the age of fourteen and began her career as a school teacher in Memphis. A self-taught musician, she was appointed music director for the Sunday School and Baptist Training Union Congress of the National Baptist Convention USA in 1916. In 1919, Campbell became the most popular gospel songwriter in America when she composed and released her song "Something Within Me."

*More about Lucie Campbell*
Other songs composed by Campbell that can be found in Baptist hymnals to this day include "Just to Behold His Face," "He Understands," and "He'll Say Well Done."

**Louis Armstrong** was born in 1899 or 1900 in New Orleans, Louisiana. He grew up listening to Dixieland, blues, ragtime, and marching tunes of the brass bands he heard playing in the city. He began playing the cornet—an instrument similar to the trumpet—during the year and a half he spent in an orphanage–reform school for black boys in New Orleans.

Armstrong began playing the trumpet when he moved to Chicago and replaced the lead trumpet player in a jazz band. He started making a name for himself as a musician when he played trumpet on a steamboat that traveled up and down the Mississippi River, stopping in cities and towns between New Orleans and St. Paul,

Louis Armstrong

**WHAT?** The coming together in one place of people with an amazing variety of talents

**WHEN?** The decade of the 1920s

**WHERE?** Harlem, New York, home to the single largest black community in the United States. Harlem attracted black people from all over the country and from many places around the world.

**WHO?** Activists and intellectuals, such as Marcus Garvey, James Weldon Johnson, A. Philip Randolph, and W. E. B. Du Bois were already living and working in New York City. The journals and magazines of the groups they represented and wrote for, such as the National Association for the Advancement of Colored People (NAACP), the National Urban League, and the Brotherhood of Sleeping Car Porters, also published the writings of writers and poets, including Langston Hughes, Claude McKay, Sterling Brown, Zora Neale Hurston, and Countee Cullen.

**WERE THERE MORE?** Yes, Harlem was also home to singers, songwriters, and stage performers, including Eubie Blake, J. Rosamond Johnson, Bert Williams, Ethel Waters, Paul Robeson, Fletcher Henderson, and "Duke" Ellington. Added to that mix were painters and sculptors, such as Selma Burke, Aaron Douglass, and Augusta Savage.

**WHY DID IT END?** The Harlem Renaissance came to an end as the effects of the Great Depression began to be felt throughout New York City and the rest of the country. People who supported the arts were less able to support their favorite writers and artists. Theaters closed as attendance shrank.

**LEGACY?** Much of the music, literature, and art created at that time continues to influence American culture to this day.

Minnesota. In 1925, Armstrong joined with blues singer Bessie Smith for a series of recordings. Smith was already a nationally known singer, and her recording partnership with Armstrong put him in the national spotlight as well.

In 1928, Armstrong and his "Hot Five" recorded the song "West End Blues." With that song, Armstrong and his fellow musicians defined the art of improvisation, or playing parts of the song without preparation and instead composing on the spot. This record changed jazz music forever as the jazz musician became an improvisational soloist.

More about Louis Armstrong

■ Beginning in 1932, Armstrong appeared often in Europe because jazz was popular there.

■ Armstrong also appeared in dozens of movies in both comedic and musical roles.

■ Songs Armstrong is most remembered for are "Mack the Knife," "What a Wonderful World," "Sleepy Time Down South," and "Black and Blue Blues."

▶▶Fast Forward to 1964:

**LOUIS ARMSTRONG**

**In 1964, Louis Armstrong's recording of his solo performance as a singer and trumpet player in the musical play *Hello, Dolly!* became the number one song on the Billboard charts.**

**Thomas A. Dorsey** was born in 1899 in Villa Rica, Georgia. By the age of twelve he was playing the blues in night clubs and gambling houses in Atlanta where his family had moved to get away from a life of sharecropping. Dorsey regularly performed with such blues singers as Bessie Smith and Ma Rainey.

In 1921, a friend invited him to attend the annual National Baptist Convention USA meeting in Chicago. While there, he experienced a religious conversion, and while he continued to perform the blues for many more years, by the end of that year he had written his first gospel song, "If I Don't Get There with You." In the 1920s, very few churches were open to gospel music because they felt it was too close in sound and style to the music of nightclubs and saloons. That thinking began to change in 1930 when Dorsey's song "If You See My Savior, Tell Him You Saw Me" was performed by Willie Mae Fisher at a session of the National Baptist Churches USA.

**Did you know...?**

On Easter Sunday in 1939, Marian Anderson performed a concert in front of the Lincoln Memorial in Washington, D.C., before an audience of seventy-five thousand people. That concert was arranged by First Lady Eleanor Roosevelt after Anderson was not allowed to sing in Constitution Hall, also in Washington, D.C., earlier that year. That hall was owned and operated by a white women's group called the Daughters of the American Revolution.

Also in 1939, Anderson was awarded the Spingarn Medal from the NAACP.

Marian Anderson

## More about Thomas Dorsey

■ Four thousand copies of the sheet music of "If You See My Savior…" were sold at the convention. Dorsey was on his way to becoming a household name in black churches, and gospel music was becoming a part of the life of more and more black churches.

■ In 1932, Dorsey wrote "Precious Lord, Take My Hand." He wrote that song after the death of his wife in childbirth and the death of their child the next day.

■ Other popular songs by Dorsey are "Peace in the Valley," "I Am on the Battlefield for My Lord," "'Tis the Old Ship of Zion," and "The Lord Will Make a Way Somehow."

▶▶**Fast Forward to 1983:**
**THOMAS A. DORSEY**
**In 1983, a documentary film titled "Say Amen, Somebody" focused on the life of Thomas A. Dorsey.**

**Marian Anderson** was born in 1902 in Philadelphia, Pennsylvania. She began singing in the choir of the Union Baptist Church of Philadelphia at age six. She joined the Philadelphia Choral Society while still in high school and began studying professionally at age fourteen.

In 1925, she appeared with the New York Philharmonic Orchestra, and she debuted at Carnegie Hall in 1928. She went on to tour throughout Europe where she performed regularly for the next ten years.

Whether singing here in the United States or abroad, Anderson always maintained a wide range of songs in her repertoire (program), from Negro spirituals to operatic arias (solos).

PHAT FACT #15
In 1958, Marian Anderson was appointed to serve as a member of the United States' delegation to the United Nations. In 1963, President Lyndon Johnson awarded her the Presidential Medal of Freedom.

The internationally famous orchestra conductor
Arturo Toscanini once told Marian Anderson,
"Yours is a voice one hears once in a hundred years."

▶▶ Fast Forward to 1955:
**MARIAN ANDERSON**
**A concert soloist until 1955, Marian Anderson then made her debut performance with the Metropolitan Opera in New York City. She performed the role of Ulrica in Verdi's Un Ballo in Maschera (A Masked Ball). She was the first African American** singer to perform with the Metropolitan Opera.

## BLACK ACTIVISTS

Nannie Helen Burroughs was born in 1879 in Orange, Virginia. Noted for her involvement in the National Baptist Convention USA, she was an early and outspoken critic of the restrictions

## The Niagara Movement

**WHAT?** A movement organized by W. E. B. Du Bois and William Monroe Trotter in 1905 for the purpose of gathering a group of black leaders from across the country to challenge the leadership of Booker T. Washington, especially relating to his willingness to give up black people's right to vote

**WHEN?** Met every year through 1909

**WHY?** The Niagara Movement had eight demands, the most significant of which were the freedom to print and promote the group's "radical" ideas; the end of segregation in all areas of American public life; a recognition of the equality of all people; the training of more blacks for the professions rather than Booker T. Washington's emphasis on industrial training; an end to discrimination in hiring; and black workers' access to the various labor unions.

**RESULTS?** The Niagara Movement was the foundation on which the National Association for the Advancement of Colored People (NAACP) was organized in 1909 and of which W. E. B. Du Bois was a founding member.

Nannie Helen Burroughs

(against drinking alcohol) movement. She also worked for fair wages for women and the banning of segregation statutes in public transportation.

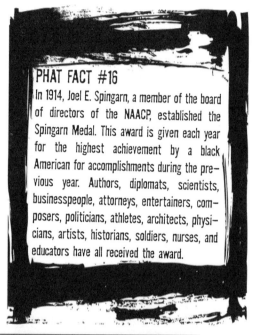

**PHAT FACT #16**

In 1914, Joel E. Spingarn, a member of the board of directors of the NAACP, established the Spingarn Medal. This award is given each year for the highest achievement by a black American for accomplishments during the previous year. Authors, diplomats, scientists, businesspeople, attorneys, entertainers, composers, politicians, athletes, architects, physicians, artists, historians, soldiers, nurses, and educators have all received the award.

imposed on women in the black Baptist church. In 1900, she joined Virginia Broughton in organizing the Women's Convention, an auxiliary of the NBCUSA. In addition to her work with black Baptist women, Burroughs was active in black and women's suffrage (right to vote) movements, anti-lynching campaigns, and the temperance

## Executive Order 8802

**WHAT?** An order that integrated war production facilities (factories) in the United States

**WHEN?** Issued by President Franklin Roosevelt in 1941

**WHY?** Issued in response to a planned march to bring one hundred thousand black people to Washington, D.C., during the summer of 1941 to protest discrimination in the armed forces and in factories that did work for the U.S. Department of Defense

**WHAT HAPPENED?** Brought an immediate end to segregation in all defense-related industries and opened up thousands of high-paying jobs to black men and women who had been shut out of these jobs before

In its 1954 <u>Brown v. Board of Education</u> ruling, the U.S. Supreme Court stated, "It is doubtful that any child may reasonably be expected to succeed in life if he (or she) is denied the opportunity of an education. Such an opportunity. . .is a right which must be made available to all in equal terms."

**Marcus Garvey** was born in Jamaica, West Indies, in 1887. He came to the United States in 1916 and became the leader of the most famous black emigration movement in the United States. He also founded the Universal Negro Improvement Association (UNIA). Through the UNIA, Garvey planned to sell shares in a steamship company—The Black Star Line—and transport blacks to Liberia and Sierra Leone where they could build a nation of their own. He published a journal called *The Negro World* with a circulation of more than two hundred thousand readers. He also ran restaurants, clothing stores, laundries, and print shops, employing more than a thousand black Americans. His movement

## Did you know...?

The planned march on Washington, D.C., in 1941 was led by A. Philip Randolph. He was the leader of a union of black workers called the Brotherhood of Sleeping Car Porters. These porters worked on trains and did work similar to what flight attendants do today on airplanes.

## NAACP Legal Defense Fund

**WHAT?** Fund created to develop ways to take cases to court that challenged segregation across America
**WHEN?** Established in 1939
**WHO?** Attorney Thurgood Marshall named chief counsel
**MOST FAMOUS CASE?** The 1954 U.S. Supreme Court ruling of *Brown v. Board of Education*, which ended legal segregation in public education

## Brown v. Board of Education

**WHAT?** The United States Supreme Court ruling in *Brown v. Board of Education of Topeka*

**WHEN?** 1954

**WHY?** Public schools in the South were segregated by law. Blacks often had to travel great distances—passing a closer school for white students—to get to school.

**WHAT HAPPENED?** NAACP Legal Defense Fund lawyer Thurgood Marshall argued before the Supreme Court that segregated schools were separate but not equal.

**WHAT DID THE SUPREME COURT SAY?** It agreed with the defense fund's argument and said that "separate educational facilities are inherently unequal."

ended when he was forced to leave the country after serving two years in jail for mail fraud—improperly raising money through the mail for his steamship company.

## Did you know...?

The NAACP was originally conceived as an organization with white leadership in almost all of its national offices. Now the group has become an organization with black leadership at local, state, and national levels. Some of their national leaders have been Walter White, Roy Wilkins, Rev. Benjamin Hooks, and former congressman Kweisi Mfume.

**A. Philip Randolph** was born in 1889 in Crescent City, Florida. Moving to New York City in 1911, Randolph studied at the City University of New York and at New York University. Rather than focusing his efforts on civil rights organizations, he believed that the American labor movement offered the most promise for black economic advancement in America. In 1925, Randolph was asked by sleeping car porters on the railroads to lead their efforts to become an organized labor group. (As explained earlier, these porters worked on trains and were similar to flight attendants today.) In 1937, Randolph negotiated a

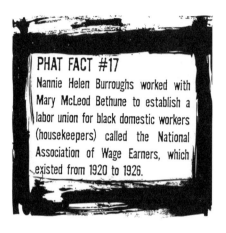

**PHAT FACT #17**

Nannie Helen Burroughs worked with Mary McLeod Bethune to establish a labor union for black domestic workers (housekeepers) called the National Association of Wage Earners, which existed from 1920 to 1926.

Marcus Garvey's most famous quote as founder of the United Negro Improvement Association was "Up, you mighty race!"

contract that allowed the Brotherhood of Sleeping Car Porters to be a union officially recognized by the George M. Pullman Railroad Car Company. This was the first time a labor agreement had been reached between a black union and an American corporation.

**Thurgood Marshall** was born in 1908 in Baltimore, Maryland. Graduated from Howard University Law School in 1933. Often working with fellow lawyer Charles Hamilton Houston, Marshall worked to transform American society through litigation and the U.S. court system. Working through the NAACP Legal Defense Fund, Marshall led the way for black Americans to obtain voting rights, break down discriminatory

## The 411 on Thurgood Marshall

■ In 1961, appointed by President John F. Kennedy to become a judge on the Second District Court of Appeals in New York, Connecticut, and Vermont
■ In 1965, appointed by President Lyndon Johnson to be solicitor general of the United States, the third highest position in the U.S. Justice Department
■ On June 13, 1967, nominated by President Johnson to a seat on the U.S. Supreme Court.
■ Confirmed by the U.S. Senate on October 2, 1967, making him the first black person ever to sit on the nation's highest court

## The 411 on Ralph Bunche

■ From 1957 to 1967, served as the undersecretary of the United Nations for Special Political Affairs
■ With UN, worked on peacekeeping missions on Cyprus, in the Republic of the Congo, on the Suez Canal in Egypt, and in a conflict between Pakistan and India
■ In 1949, awarded the NAACP Spingarn Medal
■ In 1963, awarded Presidential Medal of Freedom by President John F. Kennedy

real estate laws, and receive education equal to that of whites.

**Ralph Bunche** was born in 1904 in Detroit, Michigan. He graduated from the University of California in 1927 as class valedictorian and entered Harvard University, earning a Master of Arts in political science. He taught in the political science department of Howard University. When Bunche earned his second degree from Harvard in 1936, he became the first black American to earn a PhD in political science.

In 1941, he began working for the federal government in the Office of Strategic Services (today known as the CIA) and then in the Africa section of the State Department. He next worked on the charter for the soon to be formed United Nations. In 1950, Ralph Bunche became the first African American to be awarded the Nobel Peace Prize for his efforts in working out a peace agreement between Arabs and Israelis after the creation of the new state of Israel in 1948.

## BUSINESS AND INNOVATION

**Madame C. J. Walker** was born Sarah Breedlove McWilliams in 1867 (or 1869) in Delta, Louisiana. After her husband died, she needed a way to support her daughter and herself. She moved to St. Louis and worked as a laundress. There, she also began working on a formula

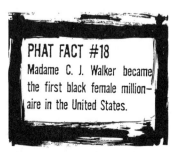

**PHAT FACT #18**
Madame C. J. Walker became the first black female millionaire in the United States.

for hair and scalp care products. Moving to Denver, she married Charles Joseph Walker. It was then that she became known as Madame C. J. Walker. They relocated to Indianapolis, and she opened a factory that produced an entire line of toiletries for the body, face, and hair. In 1910, Madame Walker opened the Madame C. J. Walker Hair Culturists Union of America, also in Indianapolis. There she trained hundreds of "hair culturists" who opened their own businesses and had hundreds of thousands of clients who bought and used Walker's products.

**Bessie Coleman** was born in 1892 in Atlanta, Texas. Migrated to Chicago sometime between 1915 and 1917. While living in Chicago, Coleman decided that she would learn to fly a plane, but

## Did you know...?

Black men had been working as Pullman car porters since the company was founded in the 1860s. Working as a Pullman porter was a prestigious position in the black community. However, it was hard work with low pay, with the men either working four hundred hours or traveling eleven thousand miles (whichever came first) before being permitted time off.

none of the American flight schools would admit a black person. With financial assistance from the publisher of the *Chicago Defender*, a black weekly newspaper, she sailed for France to begin her flight training. In 1921, while in France, Bessie Coleman became the first black woman in

## The 411 on Ida Wells Barnett

■ After moving to Chicago, organized settlement houses that aided black people who were moving to Chicago from places in the South
■ Traveled to the sites of lynchings and race riots to focus attention on those evils
■ Called for economic boycotts of white-owned businesses that discriminated against black employees or customers
■ Active in the women's suffrage movement

*Lieutenant William Powell, a member of the Tuskegee Airmen, said, "Because of Bessie Coleman, we have overcome that which was much worse than racial barriers. We have overcome the barriers within ourselves and dared to dream."*

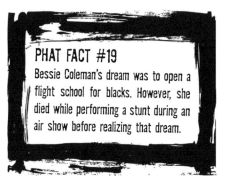

**PHAT FACT #19**
Bessie Coleman's dream was to open a flight school for blacks. However, she died while performing a stunt during an air show before realizing that dream.

the world to earn a pilot's license. She returned to the United States in 1922. To encourage more African Americans to become interested in flying, she began putting on air shows, doing various stunts with her plane in the air.

**Ida B. Wells Barnett** was born into slavery in 1862 in Holly Springs, Mississippi. In 1879, relocated to Memphis, Tennessee, studied at Rust College, then began her career writing for local Baptist newspapers. Between 1889 and 1892, she became editor of the *Memphis Free Speech and Headlight*. In her columns, she focused on the lynchings and discrimination blacks faced in America. She used her newspaper column to urge black people in Memphis to migrate to Oklahoma to escape discrimination. She also urged the boycott of the city buses in Memphis in protest of the lynching of three men in 1892. This boycott nearly bankrupted the city bus system. Her anti-lynching columns so enraged whites that her newspaper offices were burned and Barnett was run out of town. She relocated to Chicago where she continued to lead the fight against lynchings.

**Did you know...?**

In 1884, Ida Wells Barnett was thrown off a railroad car because she refused to leave the "ladies' car" and sit in the "colored section." She filed a legal action against the railroad and won personal damages of $500.

# Section 5
## Moving On (1951–)

### "We Shall Overcome"

The midpoint of the twentieth century—from 1950 through 1970—saw a level of activism and activity in the struggle for racial equality in America that had never before been experienced in the history of our nation. A demand for the right to vote, for equal education and employment opportunities, and for shared use of all parts of public accommodations ignited a groundswell of action, particularly in the South. This took the form of marches, sit-ins, demonstrations, and boycotts, as well as an increase in the use of the court system, all for the purpose of remedying the racial discrimination, inequality, and violence that had plagued our country for hundreds of years.

One reason for these actions could be traced to World War II—soldiers returned home from Europe determined to have the same freedoms they fought so hard to secure for others overseas. Another reason was that they were a natural progression of events as our nation emerged from the industrial age and propelled itself into the space age. A third reason was political: if America was going to remain the leader of the "free world," it had to lead by example, starting at home. Whatever the reasons, times were changing and America was being called to change with the times.

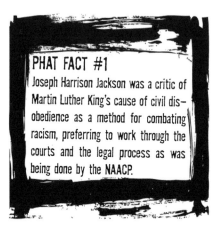

**PHAT FACT #1**
Joseph Harrison Jackson was a critic of Martin Luther King's cause of civil dis-obedience as a method for combating racism, preferring to work through the courts and the legal process as was being done by the NAACP.

## RELIGION AND BLACK AMERICA
### Preacher Power–Leading the Church

**Joseph Harrison Jackson** was born in 1900 in Rudyard, Mississippi. Ordained into the ministry in 1922. Graduated with a Bachelor of Arts from Jackson College in Mississippi in 1927 and went on to receive a Bachelor of Divinity from Colgate Rochester Divinity School in New York and a Master of Arts from Creighton University in Nebraska. He pastored churches in Mississippi, Nebraska, and Pennsylvania before being called to Olivet Baptist Church in Chicago, Illinois, in 1941. In 1953, Jackson became president of the National Baptist Conven-tion USA. He was the longest-serving president in the history of the convention, serving from 1953 to 1982.

**Samuel Dewitt Proctor** was born in 1921 in Norfolk, Virginia. Grad-uated with a Bachelor of Arts from Virginia Union University in 1942, a Master of Divinity from Crozer Theological Seminary in Pennsyl-vania in 1945, and a Doctor of Theology from Boston University in 1950. He joined the faculty of Virginia Union University in 1949 and became president in 1954. In 1960, he was named president of

## The 411 on Samuel Dewitt Proctor

■ Recruited by Presidents John F. Kennedy and Lyndon Baines Johnson to serve in a variety of jobs in their administrations
■ Director of the Peace Corps in Nigeria
■ Director of the Office of Economic Opportunity in Washington, D.C., and New York
■ Director of the Institute for Services to Education
■ Speechwriter for President Johnson and Vice President Hubert Humphrey
■ Virginia Union University School of Religion renamed Samuel Dewitt Proctor School of Theology after his death in 1997.

North Carolina Agricultural and Technical College in Greensboro where he had contacts with many of the student leaders of the civil rights movement. In 1972, after serving in the administrations of Presidents Kennedy and Johnson and in other academic positions, Proctor became the pastor of Abyssinian Baptist Church following the death of Adam Clayton Powell Jr.

**John Melville Burgess** was born in 1909 in Grand Rapids, Michigan. Earned Bachelor of Arts (1930) and Master of Arts (1931) from the University of Michigan. Responding to a call to the ministry, he enrolled in the Episcopal Theological Seminary in Cambridge, Massachusetts, where he earned a Bachelor of Divinity in 1934. He was ordained into the Episcopal priesthood that year. Over the next several years, he served in churches in Michigan and Ohio, and from 1946 to 1956, he served as chaplain at Howard University in Washington, D.C. From there he worked on the staff of the Episcopal Church in Boston for several years, and in 1970 he was elected presiding bishop of the Episcopal Church for the diocese of Boston. He held that position until his retirement in 1976.

**Katie G. Cannon** was born in 1950 in Kannapolis, North Carolina. She earned a Bachelor of Arts from Barber Scotia College in North Carolina and a Master of Divinity from the Johnson C. Smith School of Religion at the Interdenominational Theological Center  in Atlanta. She has taught at Temple University in Philadelphia, Virginia Union University School of Theology in Richmond, and Union Theological Seminary, also in Richmond. In 1974, Cannon became the first African American woman to be ordained by the Presbyterian Church (USA). Her most notable contribution is her role in the development of what is known as womanist theology. Womanism seeks to focus on the three-level forms of oppression experienced by black women in America and in many places around the world—race (black), gender (women), and income (poverty).

*More about Katie G. Cannon*

Cannon's writings on womanist theology can be found in her books *Black Womanist Ethics* and *Katie's Canon: Womanism and the Soul of the Black Community*. Other architects of womanist theology are

Jacqueline Grant, Emilie Townes, and Cheryl Townsend Gilkes, as well as biblical scholars Renita Weems and Clarice J. Martin.

**Anna Pauline (Pauli) Murray** was born in 1910 in Baltimore, Maryland. She earned a Bachelor of Arts in 1933 from Hunter College in New York City. She was one of the founding members of the civil rights group Congress of Racial Equality (CORE) in 1942. After being denied admission to Harvard Law School because of her race and gender, Murray received her law degree from Howard University Law School in 1944 where she was valedictorian and the only woman in her class. She worked a variety of jobs as an attorney, practicing law in New York, teaching law at Brandeis University in Massachusetts, and writing the amendment to Title VII of the 1964 Civil Rights Bill that outlawed discrimination in hiring on the basis of gender. After studying at General Theological Seminary in New York, in 1977, Murray became the first African American woman to be ordained a priest in the Episcopal Church.

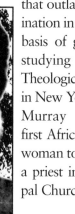

**Did you know...?**

Pauli Murphy was arrested in 1940 for failing to sit in the back of a Virginia bus (the section for black riders). She later became an author and cofounder of the National Organization of Women (NOW), one of the earliest feminist organizations in the country.

**Leontine T. C. Kelly** was born Leontine Turpeau in 1920 in Washington, D.C. She attended West Virginia State University from 1938 to 1941 but married before she could graduate. She and her husband had three children, but the marriage ended in divorce. Her second husband, James David Kelly, a pastor, encouraged her to return to college. She graduated from Virginia Union University in 1960 and taught public school until her husband died in 1969. After his death, she was invited by his congregation to serve as interim pastor of the church. It was then that she realized her calling. She attended Union Theological Seminary in Richmond, Virginia, and graduated in 1976. She was appointed pastor of Asbury–Church Hill United Methodist Church in Richmond in 1977. In 1984, she became the first African American woman ever elected to serve as a bishop in the United Methodist Church.

**Barbara Clementine Harris** was born in 1930 in Philadelphia, Pennsylvania, and graduated from Charles Morris Price School of Advertising and Journalism in Philadelphia. During her early years, she was active in the civil rights movement, working on voter registration in the South. While she was raised in the Episcopal Church, she entered the ministry only after a career in business, part of which was as an executive with the Sun Oil Company. An early advocate for the ordination of women to the Episcopal priesthood, Harris herself lacked a formal theological education. However, the Episcopal Church allowed a person to study privately with an ordained priest in preparation for ordination. That is the route she followed, and in 1980 she was ordained a priest. In 1989, Harris became the first woman to be ordained a bishop in the U.S. Episcopal Church, which is part of the worldwide Anglican Communion.

**Vashti Murphy McKenzie** was born in 1947 and raised in Baltimore, Maryland. She earned a Bachelor of Arts from the University of Maryland, a Master of Divinity from Howard University School of Divinity, and a Doctor of Ministry from United Theological Seminary

PHAT FACT #2

Vashti McKenzie is the author of a number of books, including *Not without a Struggle, Strength in the Struggle,* and *Journey to the Well.*

in Dayton, Ohio. Prior to entering the ministry, McKenzie worked as a journalist for the *Afro-American,* a black community newspaper in Baltimore founded by her grandfather in 1892. She also worked as a radio broadcaster and as a host for radio and television programs. Following her ordination as an elder in the African

Methodist Episcopal Church, she was assigned to Payne AME Church in Baltimore. In 2000, McKenzie became the first woman to be elected a bishop in the African Methodist Episcopal Church.

**Wilton Gregory** was born in 1947 in Chicago, Illinois. He attended Catholic parochial schools prior to entering the seminary to study for the priesthood. Ordained to the priesthood in 1973 by the archdiocese of Chicago, He was appointed a bishop

by Pope John Paul II in 1983 and assigned to Belleville, Illinois. He served for three years as the vice president of the Conference of Bishops. An expert in Catholic liturgical practice, Gregory earned a doctorate in sacred liturgy from the Pontifical Liturgical Institute in Rome in 1980. Gregory was elected as the first black president of the United States Conference of Catholic Bishops in 2001, serving until his term ended in 2005.

**Israel L. Gaither** was born in 1945 in New Castle, Pennsylvania. He was considering a career in the traditional ministry until he attended a Salvation Army summer camp, at which time he committed himself to an "Army career." In preparation for his career in the Salvation Army, Gaither took officer training at Gordon College and at Pittsburgh Theological Seminary. He led units of the Salvation Army in Pennsylvania and New York prior to his appointment to London, England, as second-in-command of Salvation Army international operations. In 2006, Gaither was appointed as the first black commander in the Salvation Army in the United States.

### Progressive National Baptist Convention

- The Progressive National Baptist Convention was organized in 1961.
- It was convened by Rev. L. Venchael Booth of Zion Baptist Church in Cincinnati, Ohio.
- The first issue the new convention sought to address was active support of the civil rights movement.

Rev. L. Venchael Booth

- The second was to limit the number of years the organization's president could stay in office (tenure).
- The new PNBC limited the president's term in office to two 2-year terms
- Many of the leading figures in the civil rights movement became members of the Progressive National Baptist Convention, the most well known being Rev. Dr. Martin Luther King Jr.

### Black Theology

In 1970, James Cone released his book *Black Theology and Black Power* and introduced the term "black theology" into the vocabulary and curriculum of theological discussions and education. J. Deotis Roberts offered a different viewpoint in his 1971 book

*Liberation and Reconciliation: A Black Theology.*

■ Cone wrote, "Black Theology is that theology which arises out of the need to articulate the significance of black presence in a hostile white world. It is black people reflecting religiously on the black experience, attempting to redefine the relevance of the Christian Gospel for their lives."

■ Roberts wrote, "Black Theology is a theology of liberation…. Reconciliation is also crucial. Christ is the Liberator. But the liberating Christ is also the reconciling Christ."

### Black Preaching

■ The term "black preaching" became a unique term in theological education with the release of the book *Black Preaching* by Henry Mitchell.

■ Black preaching presents revelations from the Bible so that people whose lives have commonly been touched by a shared history of racism can be strengthened and encouraged by the faith they share.

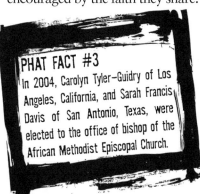

**PHAT FACT #3**
In 2004, Carolyn Tyler-Guidry of Los Angeles, California, and Sarah Francis Davis of San Antonio, Texas, were elected to the office of bishop of the African Methodist Episcopal Church.

■ Black preaching is based on the use of oral techniques. It includes a wide variety of forms and styles—no one approach to preaching can be called authentic black preaching.

### The Nation of Islam and Louis Farrakhan

■ Louis Farrakhan was born Louis Eugene Walcott in 1933 in Boston, Massachusetts.

Louis Farrakhan

■ He attended St. Cyprian's Episcopal Church and graduated from the prestigious Boston Latin School.

■ He was an accomplished violinist by his teen years.

■ Because he could not afford to attend the famed Juilliard School to continue his music studies, he enrolled in Winston Salem State University in North Carolina in 1950 on an athletic scholarship.

■ This was his first exposure to the Jim Crow segregation of the South. The experience caused him to be disillusioned with Christianity because the white people who showed so much racial hatred were also active in their churches.

■ In 1955 he heard a speech by Elijah Muhammad of the Nation of Islam and joined the organization.

■ He was given the name Louis Farrakhan when he was assigned to be minister of Muhammad's

**PHAT FACT #4**

Louis Farrakhan is best known for having called for and organized the Million Man March in Washington, D.C., in 1995. One million black men gathered for this event, which was billed as "A Day of Atonement," during which men were challenged to be more respectful and protective of black women, more responsible for their children, and more engaged in their local communities.

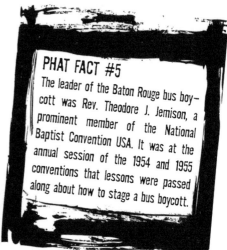

**PHAT FACT #5**

The leader of the Baton Rouge bus boycott was Rev. Theodore J. Jemison, a prominent member of the National Baptist Convention USA. It was at the annual session of the 1954 and 1955 conventions that lessons were passed along about how to stage a bus boycott.

Mosque in Boston. Following the death of Malcolm X in 1965, Farrakhan succeeded him as minister at Temple #7 in New York City.

■ Following the death of Elijah Muhammad in 1975, Farrakhan broke away from the leadership of Muhammad's son Waruthuddin Muhammad.

■ In 1977, Farrakhan refocused the Nation of Islam under the original teachings of Elijah Muhammad and began a new newspaper called *The Final Call*.

## Did you know...?

Elijah Muhammad's son Waruthuddin Muhammad sought to move the Nation of Islam into the wider community of orthodox Islam. The son changed the name of the organization from the Nation of Islam to the American Muslim Mission.

## A CALL TO ACTION
### The Baton Rouge, Louisiana, Bus Boycott
**Background**

■ In March 1953, the Baton Rouge City Council lifted the ban on segregated seating on city buses. That meant that black passengers would no longer have to pay at the front of the bus, get off, walk to the back door, get back on the bus, and sit at the rear in the "colored only" section.

■ The new law allowed any passenger to sit anywhere a seat was available on a first-come, first-served basis

■ The only restriction was that blacks would sit from the back forward and whites would sit from the front to the back. Black passengers would not have to give up their seat to a white person on demand.

■ The white bus drivers refused to work under these integrated conditions—they went on strike and demanded a return to the old segregated model of seating.

■ The attorney general of Louisiana—the state's chief lawyer who made sure the laws of the state were followed—sided with the white bus drivers and overturned the new Baton Rouge law, stating that it was a violation of the Louisiana law that required segregation in seating on public buses.

### Boycott

■ The boycott of the Baton Rouge bus service by black passengers began in June 1953.

■ Using a network of private cars, a "taxi service" was formed to provide transportation for people who needed rides to and from work or to the store.

■ The economic pressure created by the boycott on the bus company and on the city's retail stores caused the city of Baton Rouge to offer a settlement within eight days.

### The Outcome

■ While some in the black community objected, it was agreed that the front seats on both sides of the buses would remain

### Did you know...?

While the boycott in Baton Rouge lasted for only six days, it set in motion a plan for dealing with segregation in public transportation that was used in Montgomery, Alabama, for 381 days in 1955–56.

reserved for whites. The long seat at the very back of the bus would be reserved for blacks. All other seats would be filled on a nonsegregated basis.

## Montgomery Bus Boycott

### Background

■ Segregation laws in Alabama limited black passengers on public transportation to the "colored section." Under no circumstances could black passengers sit in the rows reserved for whites. When the white section was filled, black passengers seated in the "colored only" section were required to stand up so that white passengers could have their seats.

■ On December 1, 1955, that is

---

boycott: when a group joins together and refuses to use, buy, or have anything to do with a certain thing as a means of protest

Jim Crow: the practice of discriminating against black people

sit-in: a type of protest in which participants sit at a location and refuse to move

Rosa Parks is fingerprinted in Montgomery, Alabama, on February 22, 1956, two months after refusing to give up her seat on a bus for a white passenger.

## The 411 on Rosa Parks

■ Born Rosa Louise McCauley in 1913 in Tuskegee, Alabama
■ Attended high school at Alabama State Teachers' College in Montgomery, Alabama, but had to leave school to care for her ailing grandmother and mother
■ Married Raymond Parks in 1932, who encouraged her to get her high school diploma, which she did in 1934
■ A seamstress by profession but also served as the secretary of the local branch of the NAACP
■ Lost her job as a seamstress one month after the Montgomery bus boycott began in December 1955
■ Moved to Detroit, Michigan, in 1957
■ Worked as a seamstress in Detroit for several years
■ Worked from 1965–1988 in the office of Congressman John Conyers
■ In 1987, cofounded the Rosa and Raymond Parks Institute for Self-Development, a leadership organization for youth
■ In 1996, awarded Presidential Medal of Freedom by President Bill Clinton

what happened on the bus when Rosa Parks was going home from work—two white men boarded the bus, and the white driver ordered the black passengers to stand so the white passengers could sit.

■ Since the law stated that a black passenger could not sit next to or across the aisle from a white pas-

> When the police showed up at the bus to arrest Rosa Parks, she asked one of them, "Why do you push us around?" "I don't know," he answered, "but the law is the law, and you're under arrest."

senger, that meant that four black people—two from each side of the aisle—would have to stand so that two white men could sit.

■ Three black people stood up at the driver's command. When Parks did not move, the driver told her he was going to call the police. She told him, "Go ahead."

## Boycott

■ The local head of the NAACP, E. D. Nixon, called for a one-day boycott of the buses to protest Parks's arrest.

■ The boycott was called for a Monday, which allowed news of the boycott to be announced in black churches the Sunday before.

■ The one-day boycott was 100 percent successful.

■ A mass meeting was held at a local black church at which the Montgomery Improvement Association was organized and at which a relatively new minister in town, Rev. Martin Luther King Jr. was named president.

■ The focus of the boycott was no longer to protest Parks's arrest, but to inflict economic pain on the bus company and the downtown business district where blacks were the main customers.

■ The people voted for the boycott to continue.

■ During the boycott, black people in Montgomery walked, carpooled, or used a special taxi service.

## Outcome

■ The U.S. Supreme Court ruled in 1956 that the bus segregation policies were unconstitutional.

■ On December 29, 1956—381 days later—the boycott of the Montgomery bus system ended.

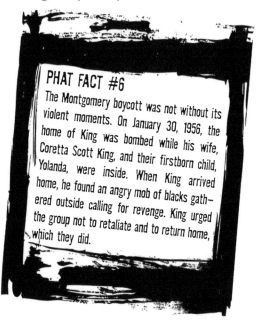

**PHAT FACT #6**

The Montgomery boycott was not without its violent moments. On January 30, 1956, the home of King was bombed while his wife, Coretta Scott King, and their firstborn child, Yolanda, were inside. When King arrived home, he found an angry mob of blacks gathered outside calling for revenge. King urged the group not to retaliate and to return home, which they did.

# The 411 on Rev. Dr. Martin Luther King Jr.

- Born in 1929 in Atlanta, Georgia
- Followed his call to the ministry and enrolled at Morehouse College in Atlanta; graduated at age nineteen
- Earned a Bachelor of Divinity from Crozer Theological Seminary in 1951 and a Doctor of Philosophy in systematic theology from Boston University in 1955
- Ministry began at Dexter Avenue Baptist Church, Montgomery, Alabama, in 1954; later became copastor of Ebenezer Baptist Church in Atlanta
- Participation in the Montgomery bus boycott launched him into leadership of national civil rights movement
- One of the founders and the first president of the Southern Christian Leadership Conference, which led civil rights protests in cities across the South as well as in several Northern cities
- Arrested several times as a direct result of civil rights activities
- Wrote the famous *Letter from a Birmingham Jail* during imprisonment in Birmingham, Alabama, in April 1963
- Involved with the leadership that planned the 1963 March on Washington, D.C., where he delivered his "I have a dream" speech
- In 1964, awarded Nobel Peace Prize for his civil rights work; second African American to receive this prestigious award
- Continued to widen his focus from the single issue of civil rights and racism to the larger problem of poverty in black and white communities across the United States
- Became a critic of the Vietnam War, believing that money needed to fight poverty in the United States was being used up by war costs
- In 1968, was planning a Poor People's March that would bring thousands of people to Washington, D.C., to address the growing problem of poverty in America
- Shot and killed on April 4, 1968, while standing on balcony of Lorraine Motel in Memphis, Tennessee

In what proved to be his last speech,
delivered on April 3, 1968 in Memphis, Tennessee,
King said, "I've been to the mountaintop,
and I've looked over and I've seen the Promised Land.
I may not get there with you, but I want you
to know tonight that we as a people
will get to the Promised Land."

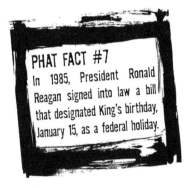

**PHAT FACT #7**
In 1985, President Ronald Reagan signed into law a bill that designated King's birthday, January 15, as a federal holiday.

## The Integration of Central High School in Little Rock, Arkansas

### Background

■ In 1957, in response to the Supreme Court ruling in *Brown v. Board of Education*, the Little Rock Board of Education approved a plan called the "Little Rock Phase Program," which would phase in desegregation over a period of time.

■ The first school to be integrated would be Central High School. However, resistance to this plan quickly emerged.

■ Arkansas Governor Orville Faubus led the charge for maintaining segregation. The governor ordered the Arkansas National Guard to prevent any of the black students from entering the school.

### Action

■ Nine students—known as the Little Rock Nine—were chosen to integrate Central High School.

■ Journalist and activist Daisy Bates was the adult coordinator who worked with the Little Rock Nine in their attempt to enter the school.

■ In spite of the National Guard blocking their entrance, the nine students were escorted into the school by a side entrance.

**Did you know...?**

Daisy Bates and the Little Rock Nine were awarded the NAACP Spingarn Medal in 1958.

President Eisenhower justified his decision to send in federal troops by saying, "Mob rule cannot be allowed to override the decisions of our courts."

■ However, a mob of angry whites rushed into the school, and the students were removed for their own safety.

■ Finally, President Dwight D. Eisenhower ordered a thousand troops from the 101st Airborne Division to Little Rock. He also "nationalized" the Arkansas National Guard, thereby making them federal troops under his command. He then ordered them all to ensure the safety of the Little Rock Nine as they attended Central High. With the protection of these troops for the rest of the school year, the students went to school, each student being protected by a soldier assigned to him or her while inside the building.

Result

■ The following school year, the city of Little Rock closed its high schools rather then integrate them.

■ The U.S. Supreme Court ruled that closing schools to maintain segregation was unconstitutional.

■ Little Rock's high schools reopened in 1959, but white families set up private all-white schools so that their children would not have to attend integrated schools.

▶▶Fast Forward to 2006:
**THE JENA SIX**

**On August 31, 2006, two black students at Jena High School in Jena, Louisiana, dared to sit under a tree traditionally known by the school as "the white tree." The next day, nooses were found hanging in the tree, in what the FBI later agreed bore all the marks of a hate crime. Racial hostilities in the community escalated in numerous incidents over the subsequent weeks, culminating in the attack by six black students (dubbed the Jena Six) of one white student on December 4, 2006. The subsequent reactions of school administrators, local law enforcement, and the judicial system were criticized by blacks and whites alike as racist and unjust in the months and years that followed.**

Did you know...?

The work of Operation Breadbasket was based on a similar selective-buying program developed in Philadelphia, Pennsylvania, by Rev. Dr. Leon Sullivan.

The Little Rock Nine, 1957

## The Sit-In Movement

### Background

■ Sit-ins had been used even as far back as the 1940s by the Congress of Racial Equality (CORE) to try to integrate public facilities. In fact, in 1957 a group of students held a series of sit-ins in parks, bus waiting rooms, hotel lobbies, and restaurants throughout that city, led by an attorney named Floyd McKissick.

### Action

■ The student-led sit-in movement officially began in 1960 when a group of four students from North Carolina Agricultural and Technical College in Greensboro sat down at the Woolworth's public lunch counter and ordered a meal. They were denied service.

They remained seated until the store closed.

■ The following days, more and more students joined the sit-ins, effectively preventing whites from being served.

■ Sit-in locations moved to other segregated locations throughout Greensboro, including other lunch counters, parks, bus stations, and libraries.

### Result

■ By the end of 1960, public accommodations in Greensboro began to be desegregated.

■ The sit-in movement spread to cities in all of the Southern states.

■ Not every city achieved desegregation of public facilities as quickly as Greensboro. In other cities, whites citizens reacted violently to peaceful attempts at desegregation.

### Freedom Rides
**Background**

■ The Freedom Rides involved black and white passengers traveling by buses on interstate highways from locations in the North to select cities in the Deep South with the intention of forcibly integrating the bus waiting rooms and defying the policies of segregation in public transportation.

**Action**

■ The first of the Freedom Riders consisted of thirteen members of the Student Nonviolent Coordinating Committee and the Congress of Racial Equality.

■ Initially they met minor resistance at restrooms and lunch counters.

■ Later the riders broke up into two groups. While in Alabama, both groups met with fierce attacks from angry whites. The police provided no protection.

**Result**

■ Freedom Rides continued throughout the summer of 1961, many of them escorted by federal marshals sent into Alabama by President John F. Kennedy.

### The 1963 March on Washington
**Background**

■ The march was originally the idea of A. Philip Randolph and Bayard Rustin.

■ The focus of the march was improving the employment opportunities for black workers in America. That was the same goal Randolph had when he proposed

## Operation Breadbasket

**WHAT?** Originally a department of the Atlanta-based Southern Christian Leadership Conference; later became a largely autonomous program with its own leadership

**WHO?** Founded by Martin Luther King Jr.; in 1966, Jesse Jackson became head of the new Chicago chapter

**WHERE?** Started in Atlanta, Georgia, and expanded in the North to Chicago, Illinois

**WHEN?** Between 1962 and 1972

**WHY?** To challenge white-owned businesses to do more business with black-owned companies and to promote their own black employees to higher rank within the white-owned companies

a similar march in 1941 that resulted in the opening of jobs in the U.S. defense industry.

■ Since the Civil Rights bill was being held up in the U.S. Senate, it was thought that a march could also help move the bill through Congress and then be signed into law.

■ Another focus of the march would be a call for the continued desegregation of public schools that had still not been achieved nine years after *Brown v. Board of Education*.

### Action

■ The March on Washington, D.C., took place on August 28, 1963.

■ All of the major civil rights groups as well as national labor union leaders and activists from the world of entertainment came together to conduct what was the largest civil rights demonstration to date.

### Result

■ More than 250,000 people gathered in front of the Lincoln Memorial.

■ Several speeches were delivered that day.

■ The march is best remembered for Rev. Martin Luther King Jr.'s. "I have a dream" speech.

### Freedom Summer, 1964

#### Background

■ The Student Nonviolent Coordinating Committee directed what

May 1961 the first Fredom Riders boarded several southbound buses. ANgry white mobs attacked them with fire bombs, rocks, and lead pipes.

was called Freedom Summer. Other groups taking part included the Congress for Racial Equality, Southern Christian Leadership Conference, the state NAACP, and other local groups.

■ White college students from Stanford, Yale, and other universities were also recruited.

### Action

■ The primary focus was enough black voter registration to have an impact in the state and national elections later that year.

■ In addition to voter registration efforts, the college students also established "freedom schools" to teach reading and math skills to black children because Mississippi had no mandatory education policies for black children. Medical teams were also dispatched.

### Results

■ Tragedy struck within the first day. Two of the white workers from the Student Nonviolent Coordinating Committee—Andrew Goodman and Michael Schwerner, both of New York City—and James Chaney, a local black volunteer, were reported missing near Philadelphia, Mississippi. After a massive hunt that involved FBI agents, their bodies were found inside an earthen dam on a farm outside of Philadelphia on August 4, 1964.

■ Other violence was directed at volunteers—both black and white—during that summer.

## Organizations

### Southern Christian Leadership Conference (SCLC)

■ The Southern Christian Leadership Conference formed under the leadership of Martin Luther King Jr., Theodore Judson Jemison, Ralph Abernathy, and others in 1957 in Atlanta, Georgia.

■ It was initially organized to coordinate the various civil rights demonstrations occurring throughout the South.

■ SCLC's mission evolved with the formation of Operation Breadbasket in 1962.

### Student Nonviolent Coordinating Committee

■ The Student Nonviolent Coordinating Committee was formed on the campus of Shaw

## Did you know...?

The term *Black Power* was popularized by Stokely Carmichael—who was then serving as chair of the Student Nonviolent Coordinating Committee—during a civil rights march outside of Greenwood, Mississippi, in 1966. He saw the term as a necessary next step in the movement once integration had taken place. Other leaders—black and white—saw the term as a call to violence, particularly during the periods of violence and uprising that gripped many urban centers during the late 1960s.

Original six Black Panthers (November, 1966) Top left to right: Elbert "Big Man" Howard; Huey P. Newton (Defense Minister), Sherman Forte, Bobby Seale (Chairman). Bottom: Reggie Forte and Little Bobby Hutton (Treasurer).

University in Raleigh, North Carolina, in 1960.

■ The main purpose of the group was to plan and coordinate the various student sit-ins that were going on across the South and in many cities of the North as well.

■ Ella Baker and Wyatt Tee Walker of the Southern Christian Leadership Conference were instrumental in organizing the group.

■ The Student Nonviolent Coordinating Committee became famous for two of the most dramatic movements of direct confrontation in the 1960s—the Freedom Rides of 1961 and the Freedom Summer of 1964.

### Black Panther Party

■ The Black Panther Party was organized in 1966 by Huey P. Newton, Bobby Seale, and David Hilliard in Oakland, California.

■ The party began as a group that was determined to bear arms publicly as a sign of its intention to use force—even deadly force—to protect its rights and the rights of other people.

■ They followed Oakland police to the scene of an investigation and monitored police conduct to be sure the officers were not using excessive force.

■ The Black Panthers also placed emphasis on providing meals for neighborhood children in Oakland.

■ In 1968, Stokely Carmichael, who was serving as the president of the Student Nonviolent Coordinating Committee, joined the Black Panther Party because he became persuaded that their message of self-defense was more effective than the nonviolent message of the older civil rights organizations.

■ Chapters of the Black Panther Party began to emerge across the country in urban centers with a similar history of alleged use of excessive police force against black people.

■ In frequent clashes with the police, one by one, the leaders of the Black Panther Party were either killed, imprisoned, or forced into self-imposed exile (living in another country).

■ By the end of 1971, the Black Panther Party had split into two feuding parties—one headed by Huey P. Newton and the other by Eldridge Cleaver.

Fannie Lou Hamer

*"I'm sick and tired of being sick and tired."*

*—Fannie Lou Hamer*

### Black Activists

Fannie Lou Hamer

■ She was born Fannie Lou Townsend in 1917 in Montgomery County, Mississippi, the youngest of twenty children of sharecropper parents.

■ Young Fannie began working in cotton fields at age six, and at age twelve dropped out of school to work full-time in the fields. In 1942 she married fellow sharecropper Perry Hamer.

■ In 1962 after hearing a sermon calling for black people in Mississippi to register to vote, Hamer traveled with seventeen other black people to the courthouse in Indianola, Mississippi, to register. When news got out about her intention to exercise her new right to vote, the plantation owners forced Hamer off land she had worked for eighteen years as a sharecropper.

■ While working on a voter registration project in 1963, Hamer was ordered off a bus with coworkers, taken to Montgomery County Jail, and brutally beaten by the police.

■ Hamer became active in welfare rights and voter registration for black people in Mississippi under direction of the Southern Christian Leadership Conference and the Student Nonviolent Coordinating Committee.

■ In 1964, she helped organize Freedom Summer, when members of Student Nonviolent Coordinating Council crisscrossed Mississippi to register new black voters.

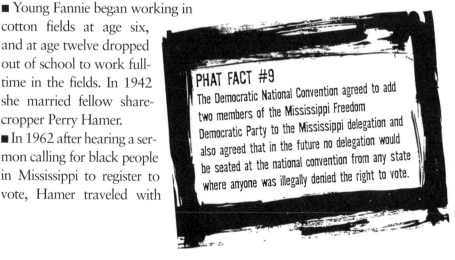

PHAT FACT #9

The Democratic National Convention agreed to add two members of the Mississippi Freedom Democratic Party to the Mississippi delegation and also agreed that in the future no delegation would be seated at the national convention from any state where anyone was illegally denied the right to vote.

Medgar Evers explained in a magazine article in 1954 why he did not leave Mississippi and the hardships there: "It may sound funny, but I love the South. I don't choose to live anywhere else."

■ Hamer was a founding member of the Mississippi Freedom Democratic Party (MFDP) which petitioned for delegate representation on the white-only Mississippi Democratic Convention. Her testimony at the 1964 National Democratic Convention was televised nationally.

■ From 1968 to 1971, Hamer served as delegate on the Mississippi Democratic Convention, and in 1972 she was elected as delegate to the National Democratic Convention.

■ In addition to her civil rights activities, Hamer helped found the National Women's Political Caucus in 1971.

### James Meredith

■ James Meredith was born in 1933 and served in the U.S. Air Force for nine years.

■ He was in his sophomore year at Jackson State University in Jackson, Mississippi, when he applied for admission to the University of Mississippi. He was denied admission because of his race.

■ Through the intervention of the state and national NAACP, a federal court in Mississippi ruled in 1962 that the university was ordered to admit Meredith for that school year.

■ There was tremendous resistance to the forced integration of the University of Mississippi. More than two thousand people came to the university to physically prevent Meredith from registering as a student.

■ To counter the mob's presence, President Kennedy sent in a force of more than five hundred armed federal agents, the National Guard, and U.S. Marshals to protect Meredith.

■ In the clashes, three hundred people were injured and two were killed.

■ Meredith remained at the University of Mississippi and graduated with a Bachelor of Arts in 1963.

More about James Meredith

■ In 1966, James Meredith set out from Memphis, Tennessee, on a

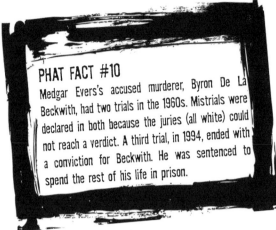

220-mile march to Jackson, Mississippi, to encourage black people in Mississippi to become registered voters.

■ Two days into the march, Meredith was shot and severely wounded by a white man named Aubrey James Norvell.

■ Other civil rights leaders joined together to continue the march, which was called the "March against Fear."

### Medgar Evers

■ Medgar Evers was born in 1925. He served in the armed forces and took part in the landing on Omaha Beach in Normandy, France, as part of the D-Day invasion that began the liberation of Europe from the Nazis.

■ He graduated from Alcorn A&M University in Mississippi in 1952. He attempted to enroll in the

law school at the University of Mississippi in 1954 but was refused admission.

■ Also in 1954, he was offered, and accepted, a position as the field director of the state chapter of the NAACP in Mississippi.

■ In the spring of 1963, Meredith announced that the NAACP was going to focus all of its efforts on the integration of all aspects of life in his hometown of Jackson, Mississippi—schools, businesses, buses, parks, theaters, libraries, and hospitals. He also indicated that the NAACP was prepared to employ every available measure in accomplishing that goal, ranging from courtroom litigation to picketing, mass meetings, marches, and boycotts.

■ That announcement, coupled with his involvement in the integration of the University of Mississippi by James Meredith in 1962, made Evers the object of daily death threats by segregation forces in that state. His home, where he lived with his wife, Myrlie, and their children, was firebombed on May 28, 1963.

■ Two weeks later, outside his home on the evening of June 12, 1963—as he was returning from his office and with his family inside the house—Evers was shot in the back and killed.

## Malcolm X

- Born Malcolm Little in 1925 in Omaha, Nebraska, as one of eight children. His father was a follower of Marcus Garvey and an organizer for Garvey's United Negro Improvement Association.

- After the family moved to Michigan, his father was killed by a hate group and his mother was confined to a mental institution.

- Malcolm went to live with his stepsister and fell deeply into the criminal life. He was arrested and sentenced to ten years in prison on multiple robbery charges.

- At age twenty, while still in prison, Malcolm was introduced to the teachings of Elijah Muhammad. Upon his release, he traveled to Chicago where he met Elijah Muhammad and was given the name Malcolm X.

- Malcolm X began organizing temples in Philadelphia, Boston, and Los Angeles and was given a permanent assignment at Temple #7 in New York City.

- He became a national spokesman for the Nation of Islam and for Elijah Muhammad and was one of the most controversial public speakers in America.

- Malcolm X's relationship with Elijah Muhammad began to unravel when Muhammad confirmed rumors of paternity suits brought against him by a young woman within the Nation of Islam. Also, Malcolm X was officially silenced as a spokesman for remarks he made concerning President Kennedy's assassination.

- By 1964, Malcolm X had left the Nation of Islam and formed his own organization. After a pilgrimage to Mecca, he experienced a conversion and changed his view that all white people were "devils" to a tone of reconciliation with all peoples. He also changed his name to el Hajj Malik el Shabazz.

- He was shot and killed on February 21, 1965, while giving a speech at one of the weekly meetings of his new organization.

## Carl Stokes

- Carl Stokes was born in 1927 in Cleveland, Ohio. He grew up in a public housing project with his mother and brother. He dropped out of school and enlisted in the army in 1945. After discharge from the military, he finished high school and received his Bachelor of Science from the University of

Minnesota in 1953. He was a 1956 graduate of Cleveland Marshall School of Law.

■ After practicing law and serving as an assistant county prosecutor, Stokes was elected to the Ohio General Assembly where he served from 1962 to 1967.

■ He narrowly lost in his first bid for mayor of Cleveland in 1965.

■ He ran again in 1967 and this time was elected mayor of Cleveland, the first black mayor of a major American city. He served two terms.

■ Stokes was elected in 1983 to his first of two terms as a municipal court judge.

■ In 1994, President Bill Clinton appointed Stokes to be the U.S. ambassador to the Seychelles Islands, located off the southeast coast of Africa.

### Jesse Jackson

■ Jesse Jackson was born in 1941 in Greenville, South Carolina.

■ He was accepted to the University of Illinois on an athletic scholarship and later transferred to North Carolina Agricultural and Technical College in Greensboro. He graduated in 1964.

**Did you know...?**

Jesse Jackson led two historic runs for the United States presidency: in 1984 and in 1988.

**Did you know...?**

Carl Stokes left Cleveland in 1972 and became the first black person to appear regularly as a news anchor for WNBC-TV in New York City. In 1978, he was awarded an Emmy Award for his work as a journalist, especially for a series of reports on Paul Robeson.

■ He became student body president as well as a leader in the sit-in movement.

■ Jackson served as field director in the southeastern region for the Congress of Racial Equality.

■ He participated in the 1965 march from Selma to Montgomery with Rev. Martin Luther King Jr. and worked with King on a desegregation/open housing campaign in Chicago.

■ Jackson enrolled at Chicago Theological Seminary but postponed his studies to devote his time to the civil rights movement (he earned his Master of Divinity in 2000).

■ In 1967 Jackson was appointed director of the new Chicago branch of Operation Breadbasket, the economic boycott and negotiating arm of the Southern Christian Leadership Conference.

■ Jackson was on the balcony of the Lorraine Motel in Memphis when King was assassinated.

■ Jackson organized his own

organization called Operation PUSH (People United to Save Humanity) in 1971.

■ In 1986, he organized the Rainbow Coalition, an organization that brought together people from all regions of the country, of all races and religions, and from every economic level to work together to reshape American social and political life

▶▶Fast Forward to 2008:
**BARACK OBAMA**
**After a historic Democratic primary campaign in which a white woman, Sen. Hillary Clinton (NY), and black man, Sen. Barack Obama (IL), were the leading contenders, in August 2008 Obama became the first African American to win the national party nomination as candidate for the office of President of the United States of America.**

## VIOLENCE IN AMERICA

**Emmett Till** In August 1955, at the age of fourteen, Emmett Till left Chicago to visit relatives in Mississippi. During that visit, Till and a group of other youths went to the local grocery store. While there, Till—and this part remains unclear—either whistled or said,

## The 411 on Alfred (Al) Sharpton

■ Born in 1954 in Brooklyn, New York
■ Known as the "boy preacher"; began preaching publicly at age four and was ordained to Church of God in Christ ministry at age ten
■ In 1970, worked with Jesse Jackson in Southern Christian Leadership Conference's Operation Breadbasket
■ In 1971, organized National Youth Movement to provide economic help for poor youth in America's inner cities
■ In 1991, founded National Action Network, which seeks social and economic justice for African Americans
■ In 1992 and 1994, led two unsuccessful runs for the U.S. Senate from the state of New York
■ In 1997, waged an unsuccessful bid for the Democratic Party nomination for mayor of New York City
■ In 2004, ran unsuccessfully for U.S. presidency

Emmett Till

"Bye, baby," to a white woman, the wife of the store's owner. A few days later, Roy Bryant and J. W. Milan went to the home of Till's great-uncle. They took Till out of the house and brutally beat, tortured, and killed him, weighing down his body with a cotton gin motor tied around his neck and throwing him into the Tallahatchie River.

Bryant and Milan were tried for murder and acquitted (found not guilty) by an all-white jury. Though the two men publicly confessed to the crime, they were never convicted.

The Till murder shocked the conscience of the entire world and helped ignite the modern civil rights movement in the United States.

**The Sixteenth Street Baptist Church in Birmingham, Alabama,** was bombed on the morning of September 15, 1963. Four young black girls were killed in the blast as they met for Sunday school that morning. They were Cynthia Wesley (age 14), Carole Robertson (age 14), Denise McNair (age 11), and Addie Mae Collins (age 14).

The bombing was a cruel reminder of the strength of white resistance to progress being made by black Americans in the areas of civil rights.

The murderers were brought to justice years after the incident: Robert Chamblis was convicted of murder in 1977 and died in jail. Thomas Blanton was convicted of murder in 2001 and sentenced to life in prison. Bobby Cherry was found guilty of murder in 2002 and sentenced to life in prison. Another suspected accomplice to the bombing died without charges having been brought against him.

**Bloody Sunday** March 7, 1965—known as Bloody Sunday—was the date when a group of six

## The Civil Rights Act of 1964

**WHAT?** The Civil Rights Act of 1964 outlawed all forms of discrimination in America on the basis of race, color, religion, and national origin. It also outlawed segregation in public facilities.

**WHEN?** July 2, 1964

**WHO?** Signed into law by President Lyndon Johnson

## The Voting Rights Act of 1965

**WHAT?** The Voting Rights Act of 1965 outlawed the various literacy tests and other methods that had been used by states to deny blacks the right to vote. It also authorized federal supervision of the voter registration process in any state where such tests had been used in the past and in which fewer than half of the voting age residents were currently registered to vote. It outlawed any form of threat or intimidation intended to prevent a person from registering to vote.
**WHO?** Signed into law by President Lyndon Johnson
**WHEN?** August 1965

hundred marchers, led by Hosea Williams of the Southern Christian Leadership Conference and John Lewis of the Student Nonviolent Coordinating Committee, attempted to walk across the Edmund Pettus Bridge in Selma, Alabama. Their goal was to march to the state capitol in Montgomery, Alabama, and appeal to Governor George Wallace to call for an end to the violence that was being inflicted against blacks and to uphold the right of black people to register and vote.

The march began outside Brown Chapel AME Church and proceeded to the top of the bridge where the marchers were met by lines of sheriff's deputies and state police who were sent by Governor Wallace. Many of the police were on horseback, and all were outfitted with billy clubs, gas masks, and tear gas canisters. When the marchers refused to leave the bridge, they were beaten, trampled, gassed, and shocked with electric cattle prods.

The national news coverage of the brutal attack shocked and horrified the country. Bloody Sunday became a decisive event in gaining national voting rights for black Americans.

**Urban Uprisings** Beginning with the 1965 riots in the Watts section of Los Angeles, other uprisings followed from 1965 to 1968 in other Northern cities, such as Cleveland, Detroit, and Newark. These uprisings were a radical departure from the message and methodology of the nonviolent civil rights movement. They also pointed to social ills in America's urban centers in the North, with school overcrowding, high male unemployment and unequal economic opportunity, and complaints of police brutality and racism against blacks.

## BUSINESS AND INNOVATION

**John H. Johnson**

■ John Johnson was born in 1918 in Arkansas City, Arkansas. He moved with his family to Chicago, Illinois, in 1933 and graduated from DuSable High School.

■ He attended the University of Chicago for two years and then attended Northwestern University School of Commerce. However, he dropped out of college to concentrate on his work with the black-owned Supreme Life Insurance Company.

■ In 1942, with a $500 loan secured by his mother's furniture, he started the magazine *Negro Digest*. His mission was to dispel many of the negative stereotypes about blacks that were found in mainstream media. The magazine also published poems and short stories of black writers.

■ In 1945, Johnson published the first run of *Ebony* magazine. From an early circulation of twenty-five thousand, the magazine now has more than twelve million monthly readers.

■ *Jet* magazine was founded in 1951, also by Johnson's company.

■ Johnson founded *Ebony Man* in 1985.

■ The Johnson Publishing Company also includes Fashion Fair Cosmetics, a book division, television productions, and the Ebony Fashion Fair, which makes donations to charities.

■ Johnson was awarded the NAACP Spingarn Medal in 1966.

■ He was awarded the Presidential Medal of Freedom in 1996 by President Bill Clinton.

■ In 2003 Howard University named its communications school the John H. Johnson School of Communications.

## Motown Records

■ Motown Records was founded by Berry Gordy in 1959 with an $800 loan from his family.

■ His first group had been turned down by another manager. He saw their potential and changed their name to the Miracles.

■ Over the next several years, Motown developed such well-known vocal groups as the Temptations, the Four Tops, the Supremes, the Jackson Five, the Marvelettes, Gladys Knight and the Pips, the Commodores, and Martha and the Vandellas. Motown also launched the solo careers of Marvin Gaye, Stevie Wonder, Mary Wells, Jimmy Ruffin, Lionel Richie, Diana Ross, and many others.

■ By 1962, Berry Gordy had launched the Motown Revue, in which he took his singers on the road to perform their hit tunes for live audiences across the country. These live appearances helped record sales and also helped establish Motown as the major black-owned recording company in the country.

■ Central to the success of the "Motown sound" was the studio band called the Funk Brothers. They provided the distinctive sound and driving rhythms that supported the vocal talents of the singers.

■ Motown also had talented songwriters who not only wrote love songs but also explored the social issues surrounding the civil rights

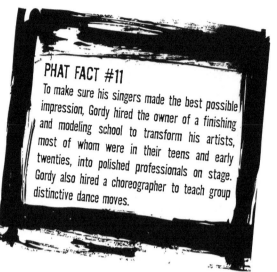

> **PHAT FACT #11**
>
> To make sure his singers made the best possible impression, Gordy hired the owner of a finishing and modeling school to transform his artists, most of whom were in their teens and early twenties, into polished professionals on stage. Gordy also hired a choreographer to teach group distinctive dance moves.

movement, the urban riots, the rise of the use of drugs in the black community, and the conflicts surrounding the Vietnam War. Some of Gordy's most well-known songwriters were Smokey Robinson (lead singer of the Miracles), and the team of Brian and Eddie Holland with Lamont Dozier. Norman Whitfield worked on many of the Temptations' hit songs.

■ In 1967 Motown Records expanded its operations beyond Detroit and opened a second office in Los Angeles. As Gordy's interest grew in expanding Motown into a film production company as well as a music recording company, the Detroit office was closed in 1972.

■ Motown Industries produced three films: *Lady Sings the Blues*, *Mahogany*, and *The Wiz*.

■ Gordy sold Motown Records in 1988, and it continues as an active recording label.

## ACHIEVEMENT IN SPORTS
### Althea Gibson

■ Althea Gibson was born in 1927 in Silver, South Carolina. Her family relocated to New York City when she was very young.

■ She showed extraordinary athletic talent, and her natural ability in tennis brought her to the attention of Dr. Walter Johnson, an African American physician who was active in the black tennis community. He became her sponsor as she played with the all-black American Tennis Association.

■ As Gibson's skill level improved, Johnson pushed Gibson into the

largely white world of competitive tennis in the U.S. Tennis Association.

■ Gibson first appeared at the U.S. Open championships played at the Forest Hills (New York) Country Club in 1950. She became the first black person, male or female, to ever appear in that tournament.

■ Gibson continued to compete at the U.S. Open each year until she won that championship in both 1957 and 1958.

■ During 1957 and 1958, she also won the British National Championship played at the Wimbledon Tennis Club in London, becoming the first black woman to win tennis championships at both the U.S. Open and Wimbledon, at which point she was ranked the number one female tennis player in the world.

■ Gibson was inducted into the Tennis Hall of Fame in 1971.

### Arthur Ashe

■ Arthur Ashe was born in 1943 in Richmond, Virginia. His mother died when he was young, and he was raised by his father. They lived next door to a park that had four tennis courts, and he began playing tennis on those public courts at the age of seven.

■ Ashe won a tennis scholarship to the University of California at Los Angeles (UCLA) in 1960.

■ By 1963, he was asked to become the first black member of the U.S. Davis Cup Team.

■ In 1968, Ashe won the U.S. Open championship in Forest Hills, the first African American male to do so.

## Did you know...?

In 1970, Arthur Ashe was denied a visa by the apartheid government in South Africa to travel there and play tennis and offer clinics to tennis players in that country. With the help of the United Nations, he finally received a visa and traveled to South Africa four times between 1973 and 1977. Using his enormous international stature as an athlete, he called for economic sanctions against South Africa as a way to weaken the apartheid system. He also led the way in having that country banned from participation in Davis Cup play. He was a founding member of Artists and Athletes against Apartheid, and he was arrested during a demonstration in front of the South African embassy in Washington, D.C.

■ In 1970, he turned professional and won the Australian Open.

■ In 1975, he won the Wimbledon championship.

■ Ashe's career ended abruptly when he suffered a heart attack in 1979 and underwent quadruple heart bypass surgery a few months later. He retired from competitive tennis in 1980.

■ However, from 1980 to 1985, Ashe was the captain of the U.S. Davis Cup team.

■ In 1983, following his second heart bypass surgery, Ashe was given a blood transfusion. This was before blood was carefully screened for the HIV/AIDS virus. Ashe contracted the virus from that transfusion and was diagnosed with AIDS in 1988. He made that information public in an announcement in 1992.

■ He became an outspoken advocate for increased funding for HIV/AIDS research throughout the rest of his life.

■ Ashe died in 1993. His body lay in state in the Virginia governor's mansion, the first person to be honored in that manner since General "Stonewall" Jackson in 1863.

### Hank Aaron

■ Henry "Hank" Aaron was born in 1934 in Mobile, Alabama.

■ His baseball career began in 1952 with the Indianapolis Clowns of the Negro Leagues.

■ Aaron was among the last black baseball players to make the move from the Negro Leagues to the major leagues when his contract was purchased by the Boston Braves in 1954.

■ He hit a home run in his first at-bat for the Braves during

*Kirk Franklin accounts for his success by saying,
"Generation X doesn't want to hear from
the reverend behind the pulpit or go to any Bible
conferences. So we need to go about getting the
message to them in another way."*

their spring training on March 13, 1954.

■ Aaron broke the home run record of Babe Ruth when he hit his 715th home run against the Dodgers on April 8, 1974.

■ By the time Aaron ended his career, he had established the record of 755 career home runs.

■ He retired from baseball in 1976 and was elected to the Baseball Hall of Fame on the first ballot in 1982.

▶▶**Fast Forward to 1997:**
**BARRY BONDS**
**On August 7, 2007, 43-year-old San Francisco Giant slugger Barry Bonds broke Hank Aaron's career home run record with his own 756th home run. The record-shattering hit traveled 435 feet.**

## THE ARTISTIC SCENE
### Kirk Franklin

■ Kirk Franklin was born in 1970 in Fort Worth, Texas. Raised by his great-aunt, she introduced him to the church and encouraged his early interest in music. He proved to be a musical prodigy and was offered his first recording contract by a local producer at age seven. By age eleven he had been appointed minister of music at Mount Rose Baptist Church in Dallas, Texas.

■ More recording opportunities came his way, and he recruited seventeen singers to work with him, calling them "The Family." His first album with "The Family" went to the top of the *Billboard* charts for one hundred weeks and sold more than a million copies.

■ Franklin's later albums have all had gold and platinum sales, making him the reigning talent in gospel music.

■ He has also worked with most of the top names in gospel and has written sound tracks for major films.

### Hip-Hop

Hip-Hop was born in the South Bronx region of New York City around 1972, and the art form

> **Hip-Hop**
>
> **What?** A musical genre and a cultural movement that encompasses the four pillars, as well as beat boxing, hip hop fashion, and (for many) political activism
>
> **Where?** Jamaica, South Bronx, and beyond
>
> **When?** Around 1972
>
> **Who?** Kool Herc, Grand Master Flash, Afrika Bambaataa (to name a few)

quickly revolutionized popular culture. What is now a worldwide phenomenon emerged from a creative convergence of individual artists who used spray paint to create visual art, turntables and microphones to create audible art, and cardboard and their bodies to create performance art.

In 1972, the South Bronx had changed from a safe and affluent community to one of the most dangerous and poverty-stricken neighborhoods in the United States. The youth in the South Bronx grew up in the shadows of the outspoken civil rights generation—and they were frustrated to realize they were still living like

*"Don't push me 'cause I'm close to the edge, I'm trying not to lose my head. It's like a jungle sometimes it makes me wonder how I keep from going under."*
—Melle Mel, "Message"

second-class citizens. They felt that they had no voice, no self-expression, and no respect or value in the world. The first "hip-hoppers" vented these frustrations creatively in musical, verbal, physical, and visual artistic expressions—what we now call hip-hop culture.

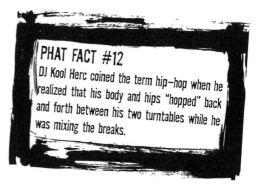

**PHAT FACT #12**
DJ Kool Herc coined the term hip-hop when he realized that his body and hips "hopped" back and forth between his two turntables while he was mixing the breaks.

### Four Pillars of Hip-Hop
- DJing (mixing records)
- MCing (or rapping)
- Break dancing
- Tagging (graffiti or spray art)

When DJs are rocking wild sets of dance music, B-boys are spinning on their heads, graffiti artists are creating stunning urban art, and MCs are rapping to move the crowd with their rhymes, that is hip-hop culture in its truest form. These essential pillars of hip-hop gave voice to a community that did not have one—a community riddled with violence, gangs, and drugs. What began as a creative mode of self-expression for individual young artists now contributes billions of dollars to cor-

porations engaged in the marketing and entertainment industries.

### Breaking It Down
Hip-hop pioneers began throwing "block parties" that featured DJs spinning records, especially funk records with heavy percussion and what are now known as "breaks." The break of a record is the portion of the song where the melody drops out, leaving just an intoxicating drum loop. That's what hip-hop dancers live and breathe for. These dancers, also known as "break-boys" or "B-boys" wait for the break to drop and then let loose their most creative moves and styles. The drawback is that this portion of the song only lasts

for approximately thirty seconds. Hip-hop DJs have perfected the art of extending the break of the record by using two copies of the same record and back-spinning the break so that it can be repeated for as long as the B-boys need.

PHAT FACT #13
The first hip-hop recording was "Rapper's Delight" by the Sugarhill Gang, released in 1979.

### Rap: Urban Poetry

While the DJs were spinning and the B-boys were breaking, MCs waited for their cue to rap during the set. In the early days, rap was very different from what it is today. The first hip-hop MCs were there to create call and response from the audience, saying things like, "Yes, yes ya'll," and "Ya don't stop," or "Everybody in the house say, 'Hoooooooooo!'" From those basic call and response lines grew a complex art form that is urban poetry, filled with literary devices and messages about the community its artists call home.

### What's Your Tag?

Tagging began on the New York City subway system where graffiti artists (aka "writers") used the train as their canvas so their work could be seen by the entire city. Writers use spray paint to place their "tag," a personal logo or identifying symbol, in as many places as possible. They get credit in the hip-hop community for the risks taken

to reach the spot they tagged, as well as the piece's visibility to the rest of the city. Writers also create "throwups," which are simply two-color bubble-lettered tags. The next stop beyond the throwup is a "piece," short for masterpiece, which is a full wall mural.

### Hip-Hop through the Decades

- **1970s:** DJ Kool Herc, Grandmaster Caz and the Cold Crush Brothers, Afrika Bambaataa, Grandmaster Flash
- **1980s:** The Sugarhill Gang, Ice T, Run-D.M.C., Salt 'n' Pepa, LL Cool J and Boogie Down Productions, Rick Rubin and Russell Simmons (the founders of Def Jam Records)
- **1990s:** Gangsta Rap—N.W.A., Public Enemy, WuTang Clan, Dr. Dre, Snoop Doggy Dogg, Nas, Jay Z, Biggie Smalls (the Notorious B.I.G.), Tupac Shukur
- **2000–present:** 50 Cent, Outkast, Lil' Kim, Mos Def, Eminem, The Roots

# Appendix
## Timeline of African American History

B. Banneker

P. Wheatley

R. Allen

| | |
|---|---|
| **1619** | Indentured Africans arrive at Jamestown, Virginia |
| **1701** | Society for the Propagation of the Gospel is founded |
| **1731** | Benjamin Banneker is born |
| **1735** | Prince Hall is born |
| **1737** | Andrew Bryan is born |
| **1739** | Stono Rebellion takes place |
| **1760** | Richard Allen is born |
| **1763** | John Chavis is born |
| **1770** | Crispus Attucks is killed at battle of Boston |
| | Phillis Wheatley is born |
| **1773** | Earliest Baptist church is founded in South Carolina |
| **1775** | Lemuel Haynes and Peter Salem fight at battle of Lexington and Concord |
| | Salem Poor fights at battle of Bunker Hill |
| **1780** | Peter Williams Jr. is born |
| **1783** | Jarena Lee is born |
| **1787** | Slavery is written into U.S. Constitution |
| | Free African Society is created |
| | Richard Allen and Absalom Jones lead a walkout from St. George Methodist Episcopal Church in Philadelphia |
| | Northwest Ordinance limiting expansion of slavery is passed |
| **1788** | Jean Baptiste Pointe du Sable establishes trading post at Chicago |

| | |
|---|---|
| **1791** | ▪ Toussaint-Louverture leads Haitian Revolution |
| **1794** | ▪ Absalom Jones organizes St. Thomas Episcopal Church |
| **1796** | ▪ James Varick leads walkout from John Street Methodist Episcopal Church in New York City |
| **1797** | ▪ Sojourner Truth is born |
| **1800** | ▪ Gabriel Prosser slave uprising takes place |
| **1805** | ▪ William Lloyd Garrison is born |
| **1809** | ▪ James W. C. Pennington is born |
| **1812** | ▪ Martin Delany is born |
| **1816** | ▪ African Methodist Episcopal Church is founded |
| **1817** | ▪ American Colonization Society is organized |
| **1820** | ▪ Harriet Tubman is born |
| **1821** | ▪ Lott Carey sails from Richmond, Virginia, to Liberia |
| **1822** | ▪ African Methodist Episcopal Zion Church is founded |
| | ▪ Denmark Vesey slave uprising occurs |
| **1827** | ▪ *Freedom's Journal* is established |
| **1829** | ▪ "David Walker's Appeal" is published |
| **1830** | ▪ National Negro Convention is convened |
| **1831** | ▪ Nat Turner rebellion takes place |
| | ▪ James Walker Hood is born |
| **1833** | ▪ American Anti-Slavery Society is founded |
| **1834** | ▪ Henry McNeil Turner is born |
| **1837** | ▪ Wendell Phillips gives first antislavery speech |
| **1839** | ▪ John Jasper is converted |
| | ▪ Joseph Cinque leads *Amistad* Revolt |
| **1841** | ▪ Frederick Douglass delivers his first antislavery speech |
| **1843** | ▪ Henry Highland Garnet delivers his famous speech |
| | ▪ Richard Henry Boyd is born |
| **1850** | ▪ Fugitive Slave Act is established |
| | ▪ Francis Grimke is born |
| **1856** | ▪ Wilberforce University is founded |
| **1857** | ▪ Dred Scott Case is heard |

S. Truth

H. Tubman

L. Carey

J. Cinque

H. Garnett

**1859** ▪ John Brown leads raid at Harpers Ferry

**1863** ▪ Emancipation Proclamation is written

▪ William H. Carney fights in battle for Fort Wagner

**1865** ▪ Thirteenth Amendment is passed

▪ Adam Clayton Powell Sr. is born

▪ Charles Price Jones is born

A. Powell Sr.

**1866** ▪ Reconstruction Civil Rights Bill is signed

**1868** ▪ Fourteenth Amendment is passed

▪ W. E. B. Du Bois is born

**1870** ▪ Fifteenth Amendment is signed

▪ Colored (Christian) Methodist Episcopal Church is founded

▪ Hiram Revels is elected to U.S. Senate

W. DuBois

**1871** ▪ Fisk Jubilee Singers are formed

**1872** ▪ William Still publishes *The Underground Railroad*

▪ Freedmen's Bureau is ended

**1873** ▪ Richard Harvey Cain serves in U.S. Congress

**1875** ▪ James Augustine Healy becomes first black U.S. Roman Catholic bishop

▪ 1875 Civil Rights Bill is passed

H. Revels

**1877** ▪ Henry O. Flipper graduates from West Point Academy

**1879** ▪ Nannie Helen Burroughs is born

▪ Exodusters travel to Kansas

**1881** ▪ Booker T. Washington establishes Tuskegee Institute

**1883** ▪ 1875 Civil Rights Bill is repealed

▪ Charles Thomas Walker begins ministry in Augusta, Georgia

N. Burroughs

**1884** ▪ Moses Fleetwood Walker becomes first black professional baseball player

▪ Isaac Murphy becomes the first African American jockey to win the Kentucky Derby. He wins that race again in 1887 and 1890

**1893** ▪ Daniel Hale Williams performs first open-heart surgery

D. Williams

**1894** ▪ Julia Foote is ordained a deacon in AME Zion Church

**B. Mays**

| | |
|---|---|
| **1895** | ▪ Benjamin E. Mays is born |
| | ▪ National Baptist Convention USA, Inc., is formed |
| | ▪ Great Migration begins |
| **1896** | ▪ *Plessy v. Ferguson* is decided by Supreme Court |
| **1897** | ▪ Church of God in Christ is founded |
| | ▪ Alexander Crummell establishes American Negro Academy |
| | ▪ Elijah Muhammad is born |
| **1900** | ▪ Howard Thurman is born |
| **1901** | ▪ Charles Albert Tindley is born |
| **1903** | ▪ Maggie Lena Walker becomes the first African American bank president |
| **1904** | ▪ Mary McLeod Bethune is born |
| | ▪ George Poage is the first African American to win an Olympic medal when he won the bronze medal in the 400 meter hurdles in St. Louis |
| **1905** | ▪ Du Bois convenes Niagara Movement |
| **1906** | ▪ Azusa Street revival begins |
| **1908** | ▪ Thurgood Marshall is born |
| | ▪ Jack Johnson becomes heavyweight boxing champion |
| **1909** | ▪ NAACP is formed |
| **1910** | ▪ Madame C. J. Walker opens hair care school |
| **1913** | ▪ Noble Drew Ali begins Moorish Science Temple |
| | ▪ Wentworth Arthur Matthew moves to United States from Nigeria and later establishes Black Jews of Harlem |
| **1914** | ▪ The NAACP initiates the awarding of the Spingarn Medal |
| **1915** | ▪ Clarence LaVaughn (C. L.) Franklin is born |
| | ▪ National Baptist Convention of America begins |
| **1916** | ▪ Marcus Garvey begins Universal Negro Improvement Association in New York City |
| **1917** | ▪ Paul Robeson is named to All-American football team |
| **1918** | ▪ Gardner Calvin Taylor is born |
| **1919** | ▪ Lucie Eddie (Williams) Campbell appears at NBCUSA |

**M. Bethune**

**M. Walker**

**C.L. Franklin**

**G. Taylor**

Harlem Renaissance begins

Fritz Pollard of the Akron Indians becomes the first African American to play professional Football

Black filmmaker Oscar Micheaux releases his first film; *The Homesteader*

**1920** Bessie Coleman is born

**1921** Samuel Dewitt Proctor is born

**1924** Roland Hayes becomes the first African American to give a concert at Carnegie Hall in New York

**1925** Malcolm X is born

Charles Emanuel ("Daddy") Grace begins his movement

**1926** Mordecai Johnson becomes president of Howard University

Carter G. Woodson establishes Black History Week

**1927** Tennis great Althea Gibson is born

The Harlem Globetrotters are organized as a performance rather than a competitive basketball team

**1929** Martin Luther King Jr. is born

**1930** W. D. Fard begins Nation of Islam

**1931** Ida B. Wells Barnett dies in Chicago

E. Franklin Frazier earns PhD from University of Chicago

**1932** Thomas A. Dorsey writes "Precious Lord"

**1933** Louis Farrakhan is born

**1935** Chemist Percy Julian develops physostigmine as a treatment for the eye disease of glaucoma

**1936** Jesse Owens wins four Olympic Gold medals

**1937** Adam Clayton Powell Jr. becomes pastor

A. Philip Randolph negotiates contract for Pullman Porters

**1939** Marian Anderson sings in front of Lincoln Memorial

**1940** Charles Richard Drew organizes blood bank in England

S. Proctor

M. Johnson

M. King

L. Farrakhan

M. Anderson

**Tuskegee Airmen**

**K. Canon**

**E. Till**

■ Hattie McDaniel becomes the first African American to win an Academy Award for her role in *Gone with the Wind*.

■ Booker T. Washington becomes the first African American honored with a postage stamp

**1941** ■ Franklin D. Roosevelt issues Executive Order 8802

■ Tuskegee Airmen are formed

**1945** ■ John H. Johnson begins *Ebony* magazine

**1946** ■ Marion Motley and three others enter National Football League

**1947** ■ Jackie Robinson integrates major league baseball

■ Larry Doby joins the Cleveland Indians to become the first black player in the American League

**1948** ■ Harry S. Truman issues Executive Order 9981

**1949** ■ Wesley Brown becomes the first African American to graduate from the US Naval Academy

**1950** ■ Katie G. Canon is born

■ Ralph Bunche wins Nobel Peace Prize

■ Chuck Cooper and two others integrate National Basketball Association

**1953** ■ J. H. Jackson becomes president of NBCUSA

■ Bus boycott begins in Baton Rouge, Louisiana

**1954** ■ *Brown v. Board of Education* ruling is handed down

**1955** ■ Emmett Till is murdered in Money, Mississippi

**1956** ■ Nat King Cole becomes the first black person to host a nationwide TV program (NBC)

■ Rosa Parks is arrested and Montgomery bus boycott begins

**1957** ■ Central High School in Little Rock, Arkansas, is integrated

■ Southern Christian Leadership Conference is formed

**1958** ■ Interdenominational Theological Center is formed

**B. Gordy**

**Freedom Rides**

**M. Evers**

**1959**
■ Motown Records is established by Berry Gordy
■ *Raisin in the Sun* premiers on Broadway and wins New York Drama Critic award as best play

**1960**
■ Sit-in movement begins in Greensboro, North Carolina
■ Student Non-Violent Coordinating Committee begins
■ Harry Belafonte becomes the first African American to win an Emmy Award

**1961**
■ Freedom Rides begin
■ Progressive National Baptist Convention begins
■ Charles Harrison Mason dies
■ Ernie Davis first African American to win the Heisman Trophy

**1962**
■ Fannie Lou Hamer registers to vote in Mississippi
■ James Meredith integrates University of Mississippi

**1963**
■ Medgar Evers is murdered in Mississippi
■ Some 250,000 people participate in 1963 March on Washington
■ Sixteenth Street Baptist Church in Birmingham, Alabama, is bombed by KKK

**1964**
■ Freedom Summer takes place in Mississippi
■ 1964 Civil Rights Bill is signed
■ Sidney Poitier wins Best Actor Academy Award for his role in *Lilies of the Field*

**1965**
■ Bloody Sunday occurs in Selma, Alabama
■ Voting Rights Act is passed
■ Los Angeles erupts with Watts Riot and urban uprisings

**1966**
■ Stokely Carmichael popularizes the term "Black Power"
■ Robert Weaver becomes the first African American to serve in a presidential cabinet as Secretary of Housing and Urban Development under President Lyndon Johnson
■ Andrew Brimmer appointed governor of the Federal Reserve Bank

■ Emmett Ashford becomes first African American umpire in Major League Baseball

■ Texas Western becomes first basketball team starting five black players to win the NCAA championship. It becomes the basis for the film *Glory Road*.

**1967**  ■ Carl Stokes is elected mayor of Cleveland, Ohio

■ Martin Luther King Jr. speaks against Vietnam War

**A. Ashe**

■ Arthur Ashe wins U.S. Open tennis championship

■ Black Panther Party leaders are killed in Chicago

**1968**  ■ Arthur Ashe wins U.S. Open tennis championship

■ The Kerner Commission reports that "America is two nations separate and unequal"

■ Martin Luther King, Jr. is assassinated at the Lorraine Motel in Memphis, Tennessee

**1970**  ■ James Cone defines the term "black theology"

■ John M. Burgess becomes first black bishop of U.S. Episcopal Church in Massachusetts

■ Kirk Franklin is born in Fort Worth, Texas

**1971**  ■ Henry Mitchell writes *Black Preaching*

■ Leon Sullivan becomes first black corporate director in US history when he is named to the board of General Motors

■ James Plinto Jr. becomes first African American to head a major US airline; Eastern

**1972**  ■ Andrew Young is elected to Congress from Georgia

■ Congresswoman Shirley Chisholm of New York becomes first black woman to run for the office of President of the United States

■ Jerome Holland becomes the first African American to sit on the board of the New York Stock Exchange

**1974**  ■ Hank Aaron establishes a new home run record

Hip-hop

A. Murray

V. Williams

**1977**
- Frank Robinson is hired by the Cleveland Indians as the first African American manager in Major League Baseball
- Hip-hop culture begins in the Bronx, New York City
- Anna Pauline Murray becomes first black female priest in Episcopal Church
- Alex Haley's *Roots* is the most popular TV miniseries in history with 130 million viewers nightly

**1978**
- Mormon Church lifts ban against black priests
- Max Robinson of ABC News becomes the first African American national news anchor

**1979**
- Arthur Lewis of Princeton University wins the Nobel Prize in economics

**1980**
- Molefe Asanti introduces the term *Afrocentricity*
- Black Entertainment Network (BET) is founded by Robert Johnson

**1981**
- Frederick Price leads church in purchasing Pepperdine University Campus

**1983**
- Womanist theology begins to emerge
- Martin Luther King, Jr.'s birthday becomes a federal holiday. It is first observed in 1985.
- Michael Jackson's album *Thriller* becomes the best selling album of all-time
- Vanessa Williams becomes the first African American named Miss America
- Guion Bluford becomes first African American astronaut to travel on the space shuttle

**1984**
- Leontine Kelly becomes bishop in United Methodist Church
- Jesse Jackson runs for president of United States

**1986**
- Astronaut Ron McNair dies on the space shuttle Challenger

**1987**
- Reginald Lewis buys Beatrice Foods to head the largest black-owned business in US history

**1988**
- Doug Williams is first black quarterback to start in the Super Bowl and he wins the MVP award

**1989** ▪ Barbara Harris becomes suffragan bishop
▪ Colin Powell appointed Chairman of the Joint Chiefs of Staff by George H.W. Bush. He is appointed Secretary of State by George W. Bush in 2000.
▪ L. Douglas Wilder is elected Governor of Virginia.
▪ Joan Salmon Campbell becomes moderator of the Presbyterian Church, USA

**1992** ▪ Mae Jemison becomes the first African American woman to fly on the NASA space shuttle

**1993** ▪ Paul Morton forms Full Gospel Fellowship Baptist Church

**1997** ▪ Tiger Woods wins his first major professional golf tournament (The Masters) by 12 strokes
▪ Violet Palmer becomes the first female referee in the National Basketball Association

**V. McKenzie**

**2000** ▪ Vashti Murphy McKenzie becomes bishop in AME Church

**2001** ▪ Wilton Gregory leads U.S. Conference of Catholic Bishops
▪ Condolezza Rice becomes the first African American woman to serve as National Security Advisor to a US President. In 2006 George W. Bush would name her US Secretary of State.

**2004** ▪ AME Church elects two more female bishops
▪ Al Sharpton runs for president of United States

**A. Sharpton**

**2006** ▪ Israel Gaither becomes head of Salvation Army in the United States
▪ Racial incidents escalate in Jena, LA

**2007** ▪ Deval Patrick is elected governor of Massachusetts

**2008** ▪ Barack Obama wins Democratic Party nomination for President of the United States
▪ David Paterson is sworn in as governor of New York

# Index

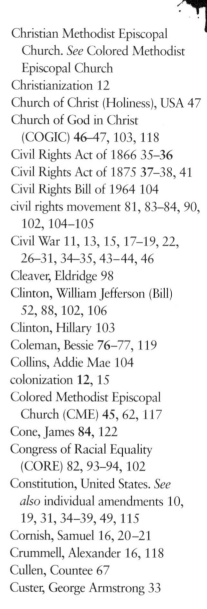